Psychology
A Level and AS Paper 1

The Complete Companion Exam Workbook

Name

OXFORD

Great Clarendon Street, Oxford, OX2 6DP, United Kingdom

Oxford University Press is a department of the University of Oxford.
It furthers the University's objective of excellence in research, scholarship, and education
by publishing worldwide. Oxford is a registered trade mark of Oxford University Press in the
UK and in certain other countries

British Library Cataloguing in Publication Data
Data available

978-0-19-842890-9

7 9 10 8 6

Paper used in the production of this book is a natural, recyclable product made from wood
grown in sustainable forests. The manufacturing process conforms to the environmental
regulations of the country of origin.

Printed in Great Britain by Ashford Colour Press Ltd

Acknowledgements

The publishers would like to thank the following for permissions to use their photographs:

Cover: petographer/Alamy Stock Photo

Photos: p17: Oksana Kuzmina/Shutterstock; **p21 & p77:** schankz/Shutterstock; **p24 &
p57:** Eric Isselee/Shutterstock; **p29 & p72:** Stephanie Zieber/Shutterstock; **p37:** Chris
Cardwell; **p47:** Roland Ijdema/Shutterstock; **p51:** absolutimages/Shutterstock; **p61:** Tony
Campbell/Shutterstock; **p67 & p43:** DenisNata/Shutterstock; **p69 & p19:** MirasWonderland/
Shutterstock; **p75:** Ekaterina Kolomeets/Shutterstock; **p83:** 5 second Studio/Shutterstock

Although we have made every effort to trace and contact all copyright holders before
publication this has not been possible in all cases. If notified, the publisher will rectify any
errors or omissions at the earliest opportunity.

Contents

Introduction

The Complete Companions series of psychology textbooks were originally devised to provide everything that students would need to do well in their exams. Having produced *The Complete Companion Student Books*, the *Mini Companions*, and the *Revision and Exam Companions*, the next logical step was to produce a series of *Exam Workbooks* to ptrovide a more hands-on experience for psychology students throughout their course and particularly in the period leading up to the exam.

Each of the *Exam Workbooks* in this series is focused on one particular exam. This first book in the series covers Paper 1 (Social influence, Memory, Attachment, and Psychopathology). Each double-page spread of psychology in the Student Book has an equivalent set of exam questions and advice in this Exam Workbook. It is designed for you to write in, so that you gain valuable experience of constructing responses to a range of different exam questions.

A distinctive feature of this *Exam Workbook* is the 'scaffolding' that we provide to help you produce effective exam answers. The concept of scaffolding is borrowed from the field of developmental psychology, where it is a metaphor describing the role of more knowledgeable individuals in guiding children's learning and development. Our scaffolding takes the form of providing sentence starters and exam tips for most questions, to help you develop the skill of writing effective exam answers. All of the material used in our scaffolding comes from the Student Book, and you are provided with page references for that book so that you can find the right material to complete the answer.

The content of this *Exam Workbook* is appropriate for both AS and A Level students, although A Level students have some additional content that AS students will not need to cover. You will be guided through the book so you will know which content is appropriate for AS and which is only for A Level.

Guide to your Paper 1 exam (AS and A Level)

AS Level
You will have one-and-a-half hours to answer all the questions in Paper 1 (7181/1). All of these questions (Sections A to C) will be compulsory. The total mark for this paper will be 72 marks.

A Level
You will have two hours to answer all the questions in Paper 1 (7182/1). All of these questions (Sections A to D) will be compulsory. The total mark for this paper will be 96 marks.

Paper 1: Introductory topics in psychology

This exam paper is divided into four sections, each worth 24 marks.

Section A Social influence
Questions can be on any of the different aspects of social influence that make up the specification (e.g. conformity, obedience, and social change). Not all topics will appear in the exam but you need to revise them all as they are all equally likely to appear. Questions on research methods, or on maths, can also be incorporated into this section, where they will be set in the context of social influence research.

Section B Memory
Questions can be set on any of the different aspects of memory that are detailed in the specification (e.g. working memory, forgetting, and the cognitive interview). As with social influence, questions testing your research methods skills and your mathematical ability may also turn up in this section.

Section C Attachment
Questions will be on the topic of attachment and the closely associated concept of maternal deprivation. As with the other sections in this paper, questions range from single mark identification or selection questions through to 16-mark extended writing questions and may include research methods questions set in the context of either real or hypothetical attachment research.

A LEVEL ONLY

Section D Psychopathology
The content includes definitions of abnormality, characteristics of different disorders, and explanations and treatments of these disorders. This follows a similar pattern to the other sections on this paper, with a mix of low, medium and high-tariff questions (e.g. 2 marks, 6 marks and 16 marks) and a mix of AO1 (description), AO2 (application), and AO3 (evaluation) questions.

Note: A Level students only; AS students answer questions on Psychopathology on Paper 2.

How to use this Exam Workbook

Specification notes
Each double-page spread begins with the AQA specification entry for this particular topic. This tells you what you need to learn and drives the questions that might be asked in your exam.

Student Book page reference
Each spread has a reminder of the pages where you can read about this topic in **The Complete Companion Year 1 Student Book.**

Scaffolding
Most questions include some 'scaffolding' to help you construct an effective response to the question. This takes the form of sentence starters or appropriate links between points. You can then flesh out this material to make a full answer.

Topic links
Sometimes you will find a link between a topic and the Student Book that we feel will enhance your understanding.

Mark box
Exam questions have different mark 'tariffs'. We have given you an appropriate number of lines in which you can fit your answer. Questions may also be AO1 (description), AO2 (application), or AO3 (evaluation), which will indicate what particular approach you should take in your response.

Questions
Each spread contains sample exam questions. This is not an exhaustive list of all the possible questions you could be asked on this topic, but it gives you the opportunity to practise answering the most common.

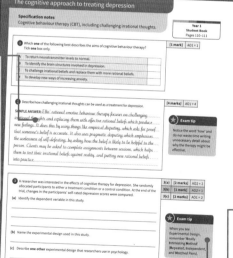

Sample answers
In some topics you will find an answer already provided. This shows you some idea of the appropriate level and length of response necessary to gain full marks.

A Level only
On some spreads we include material that is relevant only to A Level students (and is not required by AS students). This is denoted by the **'A LEVEL ONLY'** heading.

Exam tips
There are helpful exam tips throughout the Exam Workbook. These are general pieces of advice (e.g. the importance of elaborating AO3 points for maximum impact), specific guidance about how to answer a particular question, or how to avoid common mistakes when answering that question.

Essay question
Where appropriate, we have included an extended writing question. Although the question is the same for AS and A Level students, the number of marks awarded is different. We have included scaffolding for the AO1 (the same for AS and A Level students) and AO3 components. There are three suggested AO3 points for AS students and five for A Level students.

Types of AS and A Level exam question

Question type	Example	Advice
Simple selection/ recognition	*Which one of the following best describes compliance?* (1 mark) **A** *Going along with the majority because we accept their view.* **B** *Going along with the majority to gain their approval or avoid their disapproval.* **C** *Going along with the majority even though we disagree with their view.*	Questions such as these should be straightforward enough, so the trick is making sure you have selected the right answer to gain maximum marks. If you aren't sure which answer is the right one, try crossing through those that are obviously wrong, thus narrowing down your options.
Description questions (e.g. Describe, Outline, Identify, and Name)	*Briefly outline the role of the central executive and the episodic buffer in the working memory model.* (4 marks)	To judge how much to write in response to a question, simply look at the number of marks available and allow about 25 words per mark. If the sole command word is 'Name' or 'Identify', there is no need to develop a 25 word per mark response, simply identifying or naming (as required by the question) is enough.
Differences/Distinguish between	*Distinguish between an insecure–avoidant and insecure–resistant attachment.* (4 marks)	You might be tempted to ignore the instruction to 'distinguish between' and simply outline the two terms or concepts named in the question. This is not what is required, and would not gain credit. Words such as 'whereas' and 'however' are good linking words to illustrate a difference between two things.
Applying knowledge	*Simon had just returned from a motoring holiday in France, and had spent a fortnight driving on the right hand side of the road. As he drove his car off the ferry, he saw a sign saying 'Remember to drive on the left hand side of the road.'* *Using your knowledge of interference theory, explain why this sign might be helpful to people like Simon, who are returning to England after driving in France.* (4 marks)	In these AO2 questions, you will be provided with a scenario (the question 'stem') and asked to use your psychological knowledge to provide an informed answer. You must make sure that your answer contains not only appropriate psychological content, but that this is set explicitly within the context outlined in the question stem.
Research methods questions	You will be given a description of a study and then a number of short questions such as: (a) *Explain the difference between correlations and experiments.* (2 marks) (b) *Identify a suitable graphical display the researcher could have used, and briefly explain why this display would be appropriate.* (2 marks)	Most research methods questions are set within the context of a hypothetical research study. This means that your answers must also be set within the context of that study. If you don't set your answers within the specific context of the study, you cannot receive full marks.
Maths questions	(a) *Calculate the percentage of 'thieves' diagnosed as 'affectionless psychopaths'. Show your calculations.* (2 marks)	'Maths' questions can appear anywhere on the paper, and can assess your ability to carry out simple calculations, construct graphs, and interpret data, e.g. in the first question, a correct answer and appropriate working are necessary for maximum marks.
Evaluation questions	*Evaluate the 'failure to function adequately' definition of abnormality.* (4 marks)	It is important that you elaborate your evaluative points for maximum marks. We have shown you how to achieve this through the 'scaffolding' feature.
Mixed description and evaluation questions	*Outline the use of the cognitive interview and give one limitation of this approach.* (6 marks)	Not all questions are straightforward 'description only' or 'evaluation only', but may be mixed. As a rule of thumb, in questions like these you should divide your AO1 and AO3 content equally.
Extended writing questions	*Describe and evaluate the 'statistical infrequency' definition of abnormality.* (8 marks) *Discuss the role of social influence processes in social change.* (12/16 marks)	As a rough guide, 200 words would be appropriate for an answer to an 8-mark question and 300 words for a 12-mark question. If you are doing the A Level course, you may face a 16-mark question. The only difference between this and a 12-mark question is the requirement for further evaluation.
Extended writing questions with specific instructions	*Thomas has a phobia of clowns. He relates this to a scary experience he had as a child. He was at the circus when a clown jumped up from the row behind Thomas and startled him so much that his parents had to leave before the show ended. Thomas was so disturbed that he has not even been able to look at a picture of a clown since, let alone go anywhere near one.* *Describe and evaluate the two-process model as an explanation of phobias. Refer to the example of Thomas as part of your answer.* (12 marks)	Some extended writing questions not only require a discussion of a particular theory, model, etc. (i.e. AO1 and AO3), but also have an additional requirement. This example requires you to discuss not only the two-process model of phobias but to do this in the context of the stimulus material provided. Although the model is the key requirement of the question, don't make the mistake of assuming that the applied aspect of the question is less important.

The way your answers are marked

Questions and mark schemes

Examiners mark your answers using mark schemes and marking criteria. These vary from question to question, depending on the specific demands, but below are some examples.

1-mark questions: 1 mark is given for an accurate selection of the right answer or an appropriate identification. Giving the wrong answer or selecting more than one alternative from those available would result in 0 marks.

2-mark questions: For questions such as *'Identify the level of measurement used in this study. Explain your answer'*, 1 mark would be given for identifying the correct level of measurement, and 1 mark for explaining why this is the case. Other 2-mark questions such as 'Calculate the mean score from this data, and show your calculations' have two requirements (i.e. the correct answer and appropriate workings), which would receive 1 mark each.

3-mark questions: These questions might focus on a descriptive point, e.g. *'Outline one explanation of…'*, where the mark awarded would reflect the detail, accuracy, and overall organisation of your answer. They can also be evaluative, e.g. *'Give one limitation of the statistical infrequency definition of abnormality'*. The number of marks awarded in these AO3 questions is largely determined by the degree of elaboration of your critical point.

4-mark questions: Descriptive and evaluative questions can sometimes be assigned 4 marks, so will require slightly more detail or elaboration than you would write for a 3-mark question. It is useful to try to write the same number of 'points' as the marks available. You may be familiar with the PEEL (Point, Evidence, Explanation, Link) approach that involves making four different statements for a 4-mark AO3 question. Sometimes 4-mark questions are simply two 2-mark questions in disguise, i.e. they contain two specific components, each worth 2 marks.

6-mark questions: These can have very different requirements (e.g. description only, description plus application, or evaluation only), in which case their actual wording varies, e.g. you may come across a question such as *'Describe research into forgetting'* (6 marks) or *'Evaluate Bowlby's maternal deprivation theory'* (6 marks). For each of these you need to decide what is an appropriate level of breadth (how many studies for the first question, how many critical points for the second) and depth (how much detail, how much elaboration). Usually the answer is two, (i.e. describe two studies) as this is a suitable compromise in the need for both breadth and depth in these questions.

8, 12, and 16-mark questions: Questions above 6 marks are generally referred to as 'extended writing' questions. They always have more than one requirement, so examiners will be assessing (usually) both AO1 and AO3 in what is effectively a short essay response. There are four main criteria that an examiner will be looking for in extended writing answers.

Description (AO1) – have you described the material accurately and added appropriate detail? There are a number of ways in which you can add detail. These include expanding your description by going a bit deeper (i.e. giving more information rather than offering a superficial overview), providing an appropriate example to illustrate the point being made, or adding a study (which adds authority and evidence of wider reading).

Evaluation (AO3) – have you used your critical points effectively? Have you elaborated the points you have made? Examiners will be assessing whether you have made the most of a critical point. A simple way is to identify the point (e.g. that there is research support), justify the point (e.g. provide the findings that back up your claim) and elaborate the point (e.g. link back to the thing being evaluated, demonstrate how research support strengthens a theory or adds support to a research study). In this Exam Workbook we have aimed at writing 30 words of evaluation per mark available for AO3.

- AS 8-mark question = 4 marks for AO3 and so around 120 words of evaluation

- A Level 8-mark question = up to 5 marks for AO3 and so around 150 words of evaluation or 3 marks for AO3, if there are marks awarded for AO2, and so around 90 words for AO3

- 12-mark question = 6 marks for AO3 and so 180 words of evaluation

- 16-mark question = we have worked on the assumption that you would use five AO3 points of 60 words each. However, you might decide to just use four of the AO3 points we provide and expand each to 75 words. This is entirely appropriate.

Organisation – does your answer flow and are your arguments clear and presented in a logical manner? This is where planning pays off as you can organise a structure to your answer before you start writing. This is always more effective than just sticking stuff down as it occurs to you!

Specialist terminology – have you used the right psychological terms (giving evidence that you have actually understood what you have read or been taught) rather than presented your material in lay (i.e. non-specialist) language? This does not mean you have to write in an overly formal manner. Students often mistakenly believe that they have to use the sorts of words that they would never use in everyday life!

How do examiners work out the right mark for an answer?

Mark schemes are broken down into different levels. Each of these levels has a descriptor, which describes what an answer for that level should look like i.e. an average performance for that range of marks. Examiners will first choose the level they think the answer is and then use the 'magnet effect'. This means once they have decided the level, they will decide whether it is closer to the level above (pulling it to the top of that level), closer to the one below (pulling marks to the bottom of the level) or just in the middle.

Answers

All answers for this Exam Workbook can be found at:

www.oxfordsecondary.co.uk/completecompanionsanswers

Types of conformity and explanations for conformity

Specification notes
Types of conformity: internalisation, identification and compliance. Explanations for conformity: informational social influence and normative social influence.

Year 1
Student Book
Pages 18–19

---

1 Which **one** of the following best describes compliance? Tick **one** box only.

[1 mark] | AO1 = 1

A	Going along with the majority because we accept their view.	
B	Going along with the majority to gain their approval or avoid their disapproval.	
C	Going along with the majority because we want to be associated with them.	
D	Going along with the majority even though we disagree with their view.	

---

2 Explain the difference between normative social influence and informational social influence.

[4 marks] | AO1 = 4

Normative social influence is _____

_____

For example _____

However, informational social influence is _____

_____

For example _____

⭐ **Exam tip**

Whenever you are asked to explain the difference between two things, use words like 'however' or 'whereas'.

---

3 A researcher was interested in discovering the reasons why children conform to their peers. She interviewed some children about their behaviour with their peers. The questions included: 'Have you ever done what your peers did even though you knew that what they were doing was wrong?' and 'Have you ever done what your peers did because you wanted to be accepted as a member of their group?'. The children were encouraged to talk freely about their experiences, which were tape-recorded by the researcher.

3(a)	[2 marks]	AO2 = 2
3(b)	[2 marks]	AO1 = 2
3(c)	[2 marks]	AO3 = 2

(a) What was the researcher's aim in this study?

_____

_____

(b) Explain the difference between an aim and a hypothesis.

_____

_____

 ⭐ **Exam tip**

Research methods can be assessed in all of your examinations, so be prepared for them popping up anywhere!

(c) The researcher used an opportunity sample for this study. Outline **one** disadvantage of this sampling technique.

_____

_____

(d) Explain the difference between a sample and a population.

| 3(d) | [2 marks] | AO1 = 2 |
| 3(e) | [4 marks] | AO1 = 4 |

_____

_____

(e) The children were encouraged to talk freely about their experiences. Explain **one** strength and **one** limitation of allowing participants to talk freely in an interview.

_____

_____

_____

_____

A LEVEL ONLY

The researcher used content analysis to categorise the children's answers as examples of 'compliance', 'internalisation' or 'identification'.

| 3(f) | [4 marks] | AO3 = 4 |
| 3(g) | [4 marks] | AO2 = 4 |

(f) Explain **one** strength and **one** limitation of content analysis as a research method in psychology.

_____

_____

_____

_____

(g) Briefly explain **one** way in which the researcher could check the reliability of her categorisation of the children's answers.

_____

_____

_____

_____

---

4 Outline and evaluate explanations of conformity.

| [12 marks] | AO1 = 6 | AO3 = 6 |
| [16 marks] | AO1 = 6 | AO3 = 10 |

The suggested paragraph starters below will help form your answer:

- One explanation for conformity is normative social influence. This is… (AO1)
- For example, if someone… (AO1)
- Another explanation for conformity is informational social influence. This is… (AO1)
- For example, if someone… (AO1)
- One strength of the normative social influence explanation is that there is research support for it… (AO3)
- However, one problem with the normative social influence explanation is that its impact tends to be underestimated… (AO3)
- One strength of the informational social influence explanation is that there is research support for it… (AO3)
- One problem with both these explanations is that it is difficult to know when a person is subject to informational, rather than normative, social influence… (AO3)

Note: You will need some lined paper to answer this question.

 Exam tip

This question requires you to show both your AO1 skills ('outline') and your AO3 skills ('evaluate'). If a question is worth 12 marks, you will need to make 3 evaluation points. If a question is worth 16 marks, you will need to make 4 or 5 evaluation points.

Variables affecting conformity

Specification notes
Variables affecting conformity including group size, unanimity, and task difficulty, as investigated by Asch.

Year 1
Student Book
Pages 20–21

1 Which **one** of the following statements about the variables that affect conformity is true? Tick **one** box only.

[1 mark] AO1 = 1

A	Increasing group size decreases conformity.	
B	The unanimity of the group has no effect on conformity.	
C	Increasing group size increases conformity, but only up to a point.	
D	Simple tasks produce more conformity than difficult tasks.	

2 Explain how group size, unanimity, and task difficulty may affect conformity.

[6 marks] AO1 = 6

Group size is _____

_____

It may affect conformity by _____

For example, Asch found _____

_____

Unanimity is _____

_____

It may affect conformity by _____

For example, Asch found _____

_____

Task difficulty is _____

_____

It may affect conformity by _____

For example, Asch found _____

_____

 Exam tip

Always give an example to illustrate your explanation of how each of these variables affects conformity.

3 When Ruth is in her Maths class of nine students she tends to agree with the answers the other students give, even when she knows they are wrong. However, when she is in her Chemistry class of three students, she always disagrees when the other two students give an answer she knows is wrong.

Using your knowledge of variables that affect conformity, explain why Ruth is more likely to conform in her Maths class than in her Chemistry class.

One variable that affects conformity is _____

Research found that _____

_____

So Ruth is more likely to conform in her Maths class than in her Chemistry class because _____

_____

_____

[4 marks] | AO2 = 4

 Exam tip

The question asks about 'Ruth', so remember to contextualise your explanation of her behaviour.

---

4 Discuss research into conformity.

| **[12 marks]** | AO1 = 6 | AO3 = 6 |
| **[16 marks]** | AO1 = 6 | AO3 = 10 |

The suggested paragraph starters below will help form your answer:

- Asch found that on 12 'critical' trials, where the majority gave the same wrong answer on a line-matching task, the participants conformed… (AO1)
- Asch found that the level of conformity varied with group size… (AO1)
- Asch also found that the level of conformity was reduced if there was a break in the group's unanimity… (AO1)
- One limitation of Asch's research is that the findings may not be true today… (AO3)
- Another limitation of Asch's research is that it only used a limited range of majority sizes… (AO3)
- One problem with research into conformity in general is that there are cultural differences… (AO3)
- Another problem with research into conformity is… (AO3)

Note: You will need some lined paper to answer this question.

Exam tip

'Research' can mean theories or studies, so you could choose to answer this question using either Asch's study, the variables affecting conformity, or both.

Conformity to social roles

Specification notes
Conformity to social roles, as investigated by Zimbardo.

1 Which **one** of the following was **not** a feature of Zimbardo's study of conformity to social roles? Tick **one** box only.

[1 mark] AO1 = 1

A	The guards became tyrannical and abusive towards the prisoners.	
B	The prisoners had no rights at all.	
C	The guards referred to the prisoners by a number rather than their name.	
D	The prisoners were made to carry out degrading activities by the guards.	

2 Outline **one** of Zimbardo's studies into conformity to social roles.

[4 marks] AO1 = 4

Zimbardo set up _____

_____

Participants had to wear _____

_____

Zimbardo observed that the 'guards' _____

_____

He also observed that the 'prisoners' _____

_____

⭐ Exam tip

There are a lot of things you could write about for Zimbardo's study, but there are only 4 marks available, so you would need to be succinct in your explanation.

3 A social psychologist gave a number of students a description of Zimbardo's prison study. The students were asked to predict the study's hypothesis and its outcome. The findings are shown in the table below:

3(a) [1 mark] AO2 = 1
3(b) [2 marks] AO2 = 2

	Number of students who were correct	Number of students who were incorrect
Prediction of the hypothesis	122	28
Prediction of the outcome	135	15

(a) From the information given in the description above, state the total number of participants in the study.

_____

(b) What percentage of students correctly predicted the study's outcome? Show your calculations.

_____

_____

(c) What percentage of students incorrectly predicted the study's hypothesis? Show your calculations to two decimal places.

_____

_____

3(c)	[2 marks]	AO2 = 2
3(d)	[3 marks]	AO2 = 3
3(e)	[1 mark]	AO1 = 1
3(f)	[2 marks]	AO3 = 2

(d) Identify **one** extraneous variable that could have affected the results of the study. Suggest **one** way in which the psychologist could have controlled for this extraneous variable.

_____

_____

_____

_____

 Exam tip

Do not confuse an extraneous variable with a confounding variable. Page 180 of the Year 1 Student Book will help you understand the difference.

(e) Name the measure of central tendency that would be used in this study.

_____

(f) Give **one** disadvantage of using the measure of central tendency you named in **question (e)** above.

_____

_____

_____

A LEVEL ONLY

(g) What level of measurement was used in the study described above?

_____

3(g)	[1 mark]	AO1 = 1
3(h)	[1 mark]	AO1 = 1
3(i)	[2 marks]	AO2 = 2

(h) The psychologist decided to analyse the data using a chi-squared test. Apart from reference to the level of measurement, give **one** reason why this would have been an appropriate test to use.

_____

(i) The calculated value of chi-squared for the students' predictions about both the hypothesis and the outcome was significant beyond the $p < 0.05$ level. State **one** conclusion that the psychologist would have drawn from her study's findings.

_____

_____

 Exam tip

'Apart from' means use a reason other than the level of measurement!

---

4 Outline and evaluate Zimbardo's research into conformity to social roles.

| [12 marks] | AO1 = 6 | AO3 = 6 |
| [16 marks] | AO1 = 6 | AO3 = 10 |

The suggested paragraph starters below will help form your answer:

- Zimbardo conducted a… (AO1)
- Zimbardo found… (AO1)
- One strength of Zimbardo's research is that it has real-world applications… (AO3)
- Another strength of Zimbardo's research is that, while it was controversial, it was conducted ethically… (AO3)
- One limitation of Zimbardo's research is that conforming to social roles may not be as automatic as Zimbardo claimed… (AO3)
- Another limitation of this research is that demand characteristics may have affected the… (AO3)
- One issue with Zimbardo's conclusion is that it might not be mindless conformity that leads people to behave in tyrannical ways… (AO3)

Note: You will need some lined paper to answer this question.

Situational variables affecting obedience

Specification notes
Situational variables affecting obedience including proximity, location, and uniform, as investigated by Milgram.

---

1 Which **one** of the following is **not** a situational variable that reliably affects obedience? Tick **one** box only.

[1 mark] AO1 = 1

A	Proximity	
B	Gender	
C	Uniform	
D	Location	

---

2 Outline how **one or more** situational variables influence obedience.

[4 marks] AO1 = 4

One situational variable that influences obedience is _____

_____

For example _____

_____

Another situational variable that influences obedience is _____

_____

For example _____

_____

> ⭐ **Exam tip**
>
> When a question asks you for 'one or more', you can write about one variable in detail, or several variables in less detail.

---

3 Milgram conducted several studies of obedience to authority. Most of these were conducted in a laboratory at Yale University. However, in one variation, the study was undertaken in a run-down office with no obvious affiliation to Yale University. Milgram found that 65 per cent of the 40 participants in the laboratory study administered the maximum shock level, compared with only 47.5 per cent of 40 participants in the run-down office variation.

3(a)	[2 marks]	AO1 = 2
3(b)	[2 marks]	AO3 = 2

(a) How many of the 40 participants administered the maximum shock level in the laboratory and run-down office conditions? Show your calculations.

_____

_____

(b) Milgram's participants were volunteers who responded to a newspaper advertisement. Outline **one** disadvantage of using volunteers in psychological research.

_____

_____

_____

(c) Milgram could have used systematic or stratified sampling in his study. Outline what is involved in these **two** sampling techniques.

3(c)	**[4 marks]**	AO1 = 4
3(d)	**[2 marks]**	AO1 = 2

_____

_____

_____

_____

(d) Milgram conducted a pilot study before carrying out his research. Explain the purpose of conducting a pilot study.

_____

_____

A LEVEL ONLY

(e) Using information from the item above, explain what is meant by ecological validity.

3(e)	**[3 marks]**	AO2 = 3
3(f)	**[2 marks]**	AO1 = 2

_____

_____

_____

 Exam tip

The question asks you to use information from the item, so remember to contextualise your answer rather than writing a general explanation of ecological validity.

(f) After Milgram's findings were published, other researchers attempted to replicate them. Explain **one** reason why it is important for research to be replicated.

_____

_____

_____

_____

_____

_____

---

4 Discuss the role of situational variables in obedience.

[12 marks]	AO1 = 6	AO3 = 6
[16 marks]	AO1 = 6	AO3 = 10

The suggested paragraph starters below will help form your answer:

- Milgram found that the proximity of the victim and of the authority both affected obedience rates.... (AO1)
- Milgram moved the location of his study to some run-down offices. This caused obedience rates to... (AO1)
- Research has shown that uniform can have a powerful effect on obedience... (AO1)
- One limitation of research into situational variables is that Milgram's study lacked internal validity... (AO3)
- One issue is that it is claimed that females... (AO3)
- One limitation of research into the effect of proximity is that it might not apply to real-life atrocities. For example, Mandel claims... (AO3)
- The claim that Milgram's research has little modern-day relevance is challenged by... (AO3)

Note: You will need some lined paper to answer this question.

Exam tip

You must focus on situational variables (i.e. location, proximity, and uniform) and not write all about Milgram's study for your AO1.

Agentic state and legitimacy of authority

Specification notes
Explanations for obedience: agentic state and legitimacy of authority.

---

1 Which **one** of the following is a feature of legitimate authority? Tick **one** box only.

[1 mark] AO1 = 1

A	Making others feel responsible for your actions.	
B	A shared perception that many situations have a socially controlling figure.	
C	Being able to move from an autonomous to an agentic state.	
D	Demonstrating commitment and flexibility in a social situation.	

---

2 Explain what is meant by the agentic state.

[3 marks] AO1 = 3

The agentic state is when _____

_____

The agentic state can be contrasted with the autonomous state. For example _____

_____

_____

---

3 When we are queuing in a bank, we are much more likely to move to a different queue if the bank manager tells us to than if another customer tells us to.

[4 marks] AO1 = 2 AO2 = 2

Use your knowledge of why people obey to explain this behaviour.

Research has shown that _____

_____

For example _____

_____

So, we are much more likely to obey the bank manager because _____

_____

However, the customer _____

_____

Exam tip

To gain the marks here, you would need to talk about the research into obedience, with specific reference to legitimate authority. Then you would need to explain what it is about a bank manager that means we obey, compared with a regular customer.

| | [12 marks] | AO1 = 6 | AO3 = 6 |
| 4 Outline and evaluate agentic state and legitimacy of authority as explanations for obedience. | [16 marks] | AO1 = 6 | AO3 = 10 |

The suggested paragraph starters below will help form your answer:

- The agentic state is... (AO1)

- For example... (AO1)

- Legitimacy of authority is... (AO1)

- For example... (AO1)

- In the real world, legitimate authority can be used to justify harming others... (AO3)

- Accepting another person's authority as legitimate can be very dangerous. For example, Tarnow found... (AO3)

- One strength of the agentic shift explanation is that it can explain other behaviours, such as bystander behaviour... (AO3)

- One problem with the agentic state explanation is that people can revert back to an autonomous state... (AO3)

- A better explanation for obedience may be 'plain cruelty' rather than agentic shift... (AO3)

Note: You will need some lined paper to answer this question.

The Authoritarian Personality

Specification notes
Dispositional explanations for obedience: the Authoritarian Personality.

---

1 Which **one** of the following is **not** a characteristic of the Authoritarian Personality? Tick **one** box only.

[1 mark] | AO1 = 1

A	Strict adherence to conventional views.	
B	Respect for people in positions of power.	
C	A belief that rules should be changed not followed.	
D	A belief in absolute obedience.	

---

2 Outline the Authoritarian Personality as an explanation for obedience to authority.

[4 marks] | AO1 = 4

SAMPLE ANSWER: *People with an Authoritarian Personality tend to see the world in 'black and white'. They also think that social rules should be followed at all times, and are rigid thinkers who obey authority.*
This form of personality comes from being brought up with an authoritarian parenting style. Children who grow up in an authoritarian family acquire the same authoritarian attitudes, making them more likely to behave obediently.

Exam tip

Remember that 'Outline' questions are AO1 only!

---

3 'I don't know what it is about Aden', said Steve, 'but he always does whatever he's told to do'. 'I know', said Alice, 'it's because that's just the sort of person he is'.

[4 marks] | AO2 = 4

Use your knowledge of the Authoritarian Personality to evaluate Alice's claim that Aden always does what he's told to do because that's just the sort of person he is.

Alice believes that Aden obeys because of his personality. However, one limitation of _____

_____

_____

This means that Alice's claims about Aden _____

_____

_____

4 Discuss the Authoritarian Personality as an explanation for obedience.

| [12 marks] | AO1 = 6 | AO3 = 6 |
| [16 marks] | AO1 = 6 | AO3 = 10 |

The suggested paragraph starters below will help form your answer:

- People with an Authoritarian Personality… (AO1)

- This form of personality comes from… (AO1)

- According to Altemeyer's right-wing authoritarianism… (AO1)

- There is a relationship between authoritarianism and obedience. For example, Elms and Milgram… (AO3)

- There is research to support the idea that people with the Authoritarian Personality are more obedient… (AO3)

- There is also research support for Altemeyer's claim that people with right-wing views are more likely to also obey… (AO3)

- However, one problem with the Authoritarian… (AO3)

- Education level may determine obedience and authoritarianism… (AO3)

- Additionally, education level… (AO3)

Note: You will need some lined paper to answer this question.

Exam tip

Studies can be used as evaluation points provided you write about why they support or challenge things. If you don't do this, you won't receive any AO3 credit.

Resistance to social influence

Specification notes
Explanations of resistance to social influence, including social support and locus of control.

Year 1
Student Book
Pages 30–31

1 Which **one** of the following is **true** about social support? Tick **one** box only.

[1 mark] AO1 = 1

A	It reduces conformity but not obedience.	
B	It reduces obedience but not conformity.	
C	It increases both conformity and obedience.	
D	It decreases both conformity and obedience.	

2 Explain the difference between an internal locus of control and an external locus of control.

[4 marks] AO1 = 4

An internal locus of control is _____

_____

People with an internal locus of control believe that _____

_____

However, an external locus of control is _____

_____

People with an external locus of control believe that _____

_____

> ⭐ **Exam tip**
>
> Remember to talk about where people believe the responsibility for their actions lies.

3 Noah and his friends were watching a football match. Noah's friends thought the goal they'd just seen scored against their team was offside. Joe knew that it was onside, but he wasn't going say that out loud! Then, one of the group said the goal was clearly onside. When Joe's friends asked him for his opinion, he said that he thought it was onside as well.

[4 marks] AO1 = 2 AO2 = 2

Using the information in the item above, explain **one** way in which people are able to resist social influence.

One way people are able to resist social influence is through social support. This is _____

_____

So Joe had an ally when one of the group said _____

_____

_____

This means that _____

_____

4 Discuss **two** explanations of why people resist the pressure to obey.

| [12 marks] | AO1 = 6 | AO3 = 6 |
| [16 marks] | AO1 = 6 | AO3 = 10 |

The suggested paragraph starters below will help form your answer:

- One explanation of why people resist the pressure to obey is social support. This is… (AO1)

- For example, if someone… (AO1)

- Another explanation of why people resist the pressure to obey is locus of control. This is… (AO1)

- For example, if someone… (AO1)

- One strength of the social support explanation is that this can be seen in the real world… (AO3)

- Another strength of the social support explanation is that research shows it does not even have to be valid… (AO3)

- One strength of the locus of control explanation is that there is a significant correlation between locus of control and resisting social influence… (AO3)

- Another strength of the locus of control explanation is that there is research supporting it… (AO3)

- However, one limitation is that locus of control doesn't always help us resist pressure to conform. For example, Spector…

Note: You will need some lined paper to answer this question.

 Exam tip

Remember that people are usually identified as having an internal or external locus of control rather than a 'high' or 'low' internal or external locus of control.

Minority influence

Specification notes
Minority influence including reference to consistency, commitment and flexibility.

Year 1
Student Book
Pages 32–33

---

1 Which **one** of the following has been shown to enable a numerical minority to influence a numerical majority? Tick **one** box only.

[1 mark] AO1 = 1

A	Dogmatism	
B	Task difficulty	
C	Proximity	
D	Flexibility	

---

2 Outline **one** study into minority influence.

[4 marks] AO1 = 4

Moscovici *et al.* asked participants to _____

_____

_____

Moscovici *et al.* found that _____

_____

_____

_____

> **Exam tip**
>
> As only 4 marks are available here, it is important to keep your outline of the study brief and to the point.

---

3 Ten participants who claimed not to recycle their rubbish were shown a documentary film about recycling. The film contained interviews with people who spoke about what they were doing to recycle their rubbish. At the end of the documentary, the participants were asked to rate how committed to recycling they believed the interviewees to be and how likely they would be to recycle their own rubbish. The researcher was interested in whether there was a correlation between the two sets of ratings.

3(a) [2 marks] AO1 = 2
3(b) [2 marks] AO1 = 2

(a) Explain **one** difference between correlations and experiments.

_____

_____

_____

(b) The researcher found a positive correlation between the two variables. Explain how a positive correlation differs from a negative correlation.

_____

_____

_____

_____

> **Exam tip**
>
> When you are asked to 'explain the difference' between two things, remember to use words like 'however' and 'whereas'.

(c) Identify a suitable graphical display the researcher could have used, and briefly explain why this display would be appropriate.

_____

_____

_____

(d) Suggest **one** way in which the researcher could have operationalised people's commitment to recycling.

_____

_____

_____

(e) Outline **one** potential benefit to the economy of research into minority influence.

_____

_____

_____

3(c)	[2 marks]	AO3 = 2
3(d)	[2 marks]	AO2 = 2
3(e)	[2 marks]	AO1 = 2

 Exam tip

Remember, operationalisation means defining a variable in a way in which it can be measured.

A LEVEL ONLY

(f) Give **two** reasons why a Spearman's rho test was suitable to use in this investigation.

_____

_____

3(f)	[2 marks]	AO2 = 2
3(g)	[2 marks]	AO2 = 2
3(h)	[1 mark]	AO1 = 1

(g) The correlation coefficient was +0.700. With reference to the table below, explain whether or not the correlation coefficient calculated by the researcher is significant at the 0.05 level for a two-tailed test.

Level of significance for a two-tailed test	0.10	0.05	0.02
Level of significance for a one-tailed test	0.05	0.025	0.01
N = 8	0.643	0.738	0.833
N = 9	0.600	0.700	0.783
N = 10	0.564	0.648	0.745

The calculated value must be EQUAL TO or GREATER THAN the tabled value for significance at the level shown.

_____

_____

 Exam tip

The 'calculated value' is the value obtained when the test is used. The 'tabled' (or 'critical') value is the value it is compared with in order to make a decision about statistical significance.

(h) Name **one** other statistical test that can be used to determine the significance of a correlation.

_____

4 Outline and evaluate research into minority influence.

| [12 marks] | AO1 = 6 | AO3 = 6 |
| [16 marks] | AO1 = 6 | AO3 = 10 |

The suggested paragraph starters below will help form your answer:

- Minority influence is… (AO1)

- Research by Moscovici showed that… (AO1)

- Research suggests minorities must adopt a particular behavioural style of being… (AO1)

- There is research support for the idea that flexibility is important in minority influence. For example, Nemeth and Brilmayer… (AO3)

- There is a tipping point for commitment in minority influence… (AO3)

- Convincing people that dissenting minorities are valuable remains difficult… (AO3)

- One benefit of dissenters is that better quality decisions can be made by numerical minorities, for example in work groups… (AO3)

- However minority influence is not always effective because we do not process a minority's message as deeply… (AO3)

Note: You will need some lined paper to answer this question.

Social influence processes in social change

Specification notes
The role of social influence processes in social change.

Year 1
Student Book
Pages 34–35

---

1 Which **one** of the following best describes how social influence processes are involved in social change? Tick **one** box only.

[1 mark] | AO1 = 1

A	Majority influence always leads to social change.	
B	Minority influence always leads to social change.	
C	Both majority and minority influence sometimes lead to social change.	
D	Both majority and minority influence never lead to social change.	

---

2 Outline one way in which social influence research can explain social change.

[4 marks] | AO1 = 4

SAMPLE ANSWER: To draw attention to the issue, the suffragettes used educational and political tactics. They then created a cognitive conflict between the existing status quo of only men being allowed to vote, and their own position. They were consistent in their views, regardless of other people's attitudes. As they were willing to risk imprisonment and death, so their influence was augmented and became more powerful. Several years afterwards, women were given permission to vote, and at this point the idea had spread to the majority.

 Exam tip

You can write about research into majority influence, or minority influence, here. Whichever you choose, you will need to explain how the research has led to widespread social change, so an example of social change will be required.

---

3 A researcher placed an advertisement in a local newspaper asking for volunteers for a study into mobile phone use while driving. The researcher selected 20 participants who said they regularly sent and read texts while driving. When asked to explain their behaviour, all ten claimed that they were doing what they believed over 90 per cent of drivers do. The researcher hypothesised that exposing these participants to a simple factual message that only five per cent of drivers send or read text messages while driving would lead to them being less likely to continue that behaviour. A month later, the participants were asked about their use of a mobile phone while driving. Their responses are shown below.

[2 marks] | AO2 = 2

	'No change'	'Increase'	'Decrease'
No. of participants	1	4	15

(a) Was the researcher's hypothesis directional or non-directional? Explain your answer.

_____

_____

_____

Exam tip

Remember a directional hypothesis states the expected direction of the results.

(b) Outline **one** ethical issue that might have occurred in this study, and explain how the researcher could have dealt with this issue.

3(b)	[4 marks]	AO2 = 4
3(c)	[2 marks]	AO2 = 2
3(d)	[2 marks]	AO2 = 2
3(e)	[2 marks]	AO1 = 2

_____

_____

_____

_____

_____

(c) What percentage of participants reported no change in their mobile phone use while driving? Show your calculations.

_____

_____

(d) The researcher decided to see if there had been a significant change in mobile phone use while driving following exposure to the simple factual message. She used the sign test to do this. Calculate the sign test value of *s* for the data shown in the table above. Explain how you reached your answer.

_____

_____

(e) With reference to the critical values in the table below, and your answer to **question (a)**, explain whether the value of *s* you calculated in **question (d)** is significant at the 0.05 level.

Level of significance for a one-tailed test	0.05	0.025	0.01
Level of significance for a two-tailed test	0.10	0.05	0.02
N = 18	5	4	3
N = 19	5	4	4
N = 20	5	5	4

The calculated value must be EQUAL TO or LESS THAN the tabled value for significance at the level shown.

Exam tip

The 'calculated value' is the value obtained when the test is used. The 'tabled' (or 'critical') value is the value it is compared with in order to make a decision about statistical significance.

_____

_____

_____

(f) Identify the level of measurement used in this study. Explain your answer.

3(f)	[2 marks]	AO2 = 2
3(g)	[1 mark]	AO1 = 1

_____

_____

(g) Name **one** other statistical test that researchers could use to analyse data at the level of measurement you identified in **question (f)**.

_____

(h) The researcher decided to interview the four participants who reported using their mobile phones more after being exposed to the factual message. Explain how she could carry out thematic analysis of her interviews.

[3 marks] AO2 = 3

_____

_____

_____

_____

[12 marks]	AO1 = 6	AO3 = 6
[16 marks]	AO1 = 6	AO3 = 10

4 Discuss the role of social influence processes in social change.

The suggested paragraph starters below will help form your answer:

- There can be social change as a result of majority influence. For example… (AO1)

- There can also be social change as a result of minority influence. To do this, the minority need to… (AO1)

- However, research suggests that social change does not always happen after social norms interventions. For example, DeJong et al… (AO3)

- Another problem with social change interventions is that the opposite effect to what was intended can occur… (AO3)

- Another issue is that research has found behaviour is based more on what people think others do, rather than what they really do… (AO3)

- One problem with social change as a result of minority influence is that it happens gradually… (AO3)

- A second problem with social change as the result of minority influence is that minority groups are considered deviant, which limits their effectiveness… (AO3)

Note: You will need some lined paper to answer this question.

Short- and long-term memory

Specification notes
Features of short- and long-term memory: coding, capacity, and duration.

Year 1
Student Book
Pages 44–45

---

1 Below are four statements about coding in long-term memory.
Which **one** statement is correct? Tick **one** box only.

[1 mark] | AO1 = 1

A	Most of the coding is acoustic in nature.	
B	Verbal material is encoded semantically.	
C	Iconic coding does not occur.	
D	Coding has a limited duration.	

---

2 Outline **one** study that has investigated the capacity of short-term memory.

[4 marks] | AO1 = 4

Jacobs studied the capacity of short term memory using the forward digit span technique. He asked participants to _____

_____

Jacobs found that _____

_____

Exam tip

You need to write about how the study was undertaken and what was found to gain full marks on this question.

---

3 Luke was looking at a picture of his old school football team, which was taken over 50 years ago. Much to his surprise, he found he could recall the names of all but one member of the team.

Use your knowledge of research into the duration of long-term memory to explain why Luke should not be surprised by how much he could remember.

[4 marks] | AO2 = 4

SAMPLE ANSWER: *Research into the duration of long-term memory has found that we can remember significant information for up to a lifetime. For example, Bahrick et al. found that people were 70 per cent accurate at photo recognition after 48 years. Therefore, Luke should not be surprised he could recall almost all the names of his old school football team, particularly if he had been a member of this team, and played alongside them.*

Exam tip

The question asks about 'Luke', and you will only gain full marks if your answer is contextualised, as it has been here.

4 Outline and evaluate research into the duration of short-term memory.

[8 marks] | AO1 = 3 | AO3 = 5

Peterson and Peterson conducted a study in which _____
_____

They found that _____
_____

This finding appears to show that _____
_____

One strength of this research is that it is conducted under laboratory conditions _____
_____
_____
_____

However, a weakness of this research is that laboratories _____
_____
_____

Exam tip

Remember that the question is only about STM, so writing about research into the duration of LTM will receive no credit.

The multi-store model of memory

Specification notes

The multi-store model of memory: sensory register, short-term memory, and long-term memory.

---

1 Complete the following statement about the sensory register. Tick **one** box only.

[1 mark] AO1 = 1

The sensory register:

A	holds information for an unlimited amount of time.	
B	is where information is held at each of the senses.	
C	transfers all the information it receives to short-term memory.	

Topic link

The multi-store model is an example of a theoretical model. You can read more about these on pages 130–131 of the Year 1 Student Book.

---

2 Explain **one** limitation of the multi-store model.

[4 marks] AO3 = 4

One limitation of the multi-store model is that STM and LTM might not be separate stores.

For example, Logie suggested that _____

_____

Furthermore, Ruchkin *et al.* found that _____

_____

This suggests that _____

_____

Exam tip

It is perfectly acceptable to use a study (e.g. Ruchkin et al.) to support the limitation you have chosen to write about.

---

3 Jack and Billie were learning their lines for the school play. 'I can't seem to learn my lines, no matter how many times I say them' said Jack. Billie said, 'I learned mine after reading them once.'

[4 marks] AO2 = 4

Use Jack and Billie's experiences to briefly evaluate the multi-store model of memory.

The multi-store model says _____

_____

However, one criticism of the MSM is _____

_____

This can be seen when Jack says _____

_____

It can also be seen when Billie says _____

_____

4 Outline and evaluate the multi-store model of memory.

[12 marks]	AO1 = 6	AO3 = 6
[16 marks]	AO1 = 6	AO3 = 10

The suggested paragraph starters below will help form your answer:

- The multi-store model says that information enters and goes to the sensory register. If we pay attention it will move to STM, which has a capacity/duration of... and information is coded... (AO1)

- Information will stay in STM for... unless it is rehearsed. If it is rehearsed it will transfer to LTM which has a capacity/duration of... and information is coded... (AO1)

- One strength of this research is that there is research support for it. For example, case studies... (AO3)

- Another strength of this model is that it is supported by case studies... (AO3)

- A weakness of this research is that it is too simplistic. For example, the multi-store model suggests that both STM and LTM are single 'unitary' stores... (AO3)

- Another weakness is that creating long-term memories involves more than just maintenance rehearsal. For example, Craik and Lockhart suggest... (AO3)

- A final weakness of this model is that STM and LTM might not be separate stores... (AO3)

Note: You will need some lined paper to answer this question.

 Exam tip

If a question is worth 12 marks, you will need to make at least 3 sustained evaluation points. If a question is worth 16 marks, you will need to make 4 or 5 sustained evaluation points.

 Topic link

You can find more information on case studies on pages 208–209 of the Year 1 Student Book.

The working memory model

Specification notes

The central executive, phonological loop, visuo-spatial sketchpad, and episodic buffer. Features of the model: coding and capacity.

---

1 Below are four statements about the central executive.
Which **one** statement is correct? Tick **one** box only.

[1 mark]   AO1 = 1

A	The central executive consists of several storage systems.	
B	The central executive directs the brain's resources to the sensory register.	
C	The central executive delegates information to various 'sub-systems'.	
D	The visual cache is an important part of the central executive.	

Topic link

The working memory model is an example of a theoretical model. You can read more about these on pages 130–131 of the Year 1 Student Book.

---

2 Briefly outline the role of the central executive and the episodic buffer in the working memory model.

[4 marks]   AO1 = 4

The central executive's function is to _____

_____

It does this by sending information to _____

_____

The episodic buffer integrates information from _____

_____

It also sends information to _____

_____

Exam tip

There are two marks available for each component. For each one, you will get one mark for a brief outline and a second mark for elaboration, or an example of how the component might be used.

---

3 A researcher predicted that participants who do two simultaneous tasks involving the same component of working memory will perform worse than if both were done separately. She was going to test her prediction using psychology students who had recently completed a course on human memory, but realised that this could lead to demand characteristics occurring. Instead, she selected every fifth name from a list of students who were not studying psychology. The researcher tested the reliability of her findings by repeating the experiment with them a month later.

3(a)   [2 marks]   AO2 = 2
3(b)   [2 marks]   AO1 = 2

(a) Is the researcher's prediction directional or non-directional? Explain your answer.

_____

_____

_____

(b) What is meant by the term demand characteristics?

_____

_____

_____

Exam tip

In this question you do not need to link your answer to the information in the item!

3(c)	**[1 mark]**	AO2 = 1
3(d)	**[2 marks]**	AO3 = 2
3(e)	**[2 marks]**	AO1 = 2

(c) Name the sampling method used by the researcher.

_____

(d) Outline **one** disadvantage of the sampling method used by the researcher.

_____

_____

_____

(e) The researcher attempted to publish her findings in a psychology journal which uses peer review. Give **one** reason why it is important for research to undergo a peer review process.

_____

_____

_____

A LEVEL ONLY

3(f)	**[1 mark]**	AO1 = 1
3(g)	**[1 mark]**	AO2 = 1
3(h)	**[4 marks]**	AO1 = 4

(f) What does reliability mean in the context of psychological research?

_____

(g) Identify the way of assessing reliability used by the researcher in her study.

_____

(h) The researcher believed her study was valid. Identify and briefly explain **two** types of validity in psychological research.

_____

_____

_____

_____

_____

[12 marks]	AO1 = 6	AO3 = 6
[16 marks]	AO1 = 6	AO3 = 10

4 Outline and evaluate research into the working memory model.

The suggested paragraph starters below will help form your answer:

- The working memory model says STM has a number of different components. One of these is the central executive, whose function is... (AO1)
- The phonological loop deals with... (AO1)
- The visuo-spatial sketchpad deals with... (AO1)
- The episodic buffer integrates information from... (AO1)
- One strength of the working memory model is that there is research support for it, such as Shallice and Warrington's case study of KF... (AO3)
- Another strength of the working memory model comes from dual task studies... (AO3)
- A third strength of the working memory model comes from evidence for the phonological loop and the visuo-spatial sketchpad... (AO3)
- One criticism of the working memory model is that the central executive... (AO3)
- One problem with supporting evidence for the working memory model comes from research using brain-damaged patients... (AO3)

Note: You will need some lined paper to answer this question.

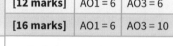

★ **Exam tip**

You need to write about the processes involved as well as describing the components of the working memory model.

Specification notes
Episodic, semantic, and procedural long-term memory.

---

1 Below are four statements about episodic memory. Which **one** statement is correct? Tick **one** box only.

[1 mark] | AO1 = 1

A	Episodic memory is concerned with skills, such as tying a shoelace.	
B	Episodic memory is concerned with knowledge that is shared by everyone.	
C	Episodic memory consists of semantic and procedural memory.	
D	Episodic memory is concerned with personal experience.	

---

2 Distinguish between procedural and semantic LTM.

[3 marks] | AO1 = 3

Procedural LTM is concerned with knowing _____

_____

However, semantic LTM is concerned with knowing _____

_____

For example _____

_____

⭐ **Exam tip**

When you are asked to 'distinguish' it means 'explain a difference' so use words like 'whereas' or 'however'.

---

3 Sarah is very good at shuffling a pack of cards. She remembers happy days with her grandfather learning all kinds of card tricks. But her grandfather is no use when it comes to learning psychological terminology. She needs a textbook for that.

[4 marks] | AO1 = 2 | AO2 = 2

Identify two types of long-term memory and explain how both types are shown in the passage above.

One type of long-term memory is _____

_____

This is shown when Sarah _____

_____

Another type of long-term memory is _____

_____

This is shown when Sarah _____

_____

_____

4 Outline and evaluate semantic and procedural long-term memory.

[8 marks] AO1 = 3 AO3 = 5

Semantic memory is _____

_____

For example _____

_____

Procedural memory involves _____

_____

For example _____

_____

There is research support for the different types of LTM. For example, the case study
of HM _____

_____

_____

_____

However, one criticism of research into types of LTM is the use of patients with brain
damage _____

_____

_____

_____

 Exam tip

You could also write
about episodic memory,
provided you used it in an
evaluative rather than a
descriptive way.

Specification notes
Proactive and retroactive interference.

Year 1
Student Book
Pages 52–53

[1 mark] | AO1 = 1

1 Below are four statements about interference as an explanation for forgetting. Which **one** statement is **false**? Tick **one** box only.

A	There is no experimental support for interference theory.	
B	There are two types of interference.	
C	Interference is most likely when things we have to remember are similar.	
D	Interference can explain forgetting from both STM and LTM.	

[4 marks] | AO1 = 4

2 Explain the difference between proactive and retroactive interference.

SAMPLE ANSWER: *Proactive interference is when past learning interferes with more recent learning. For example, learning to drive an automatic car first, and then forgetting to change gear when driving a manual car later.*
Retroactive interference is when recent learning interferes with past learning. For example, learning Spanish first then learning French later, and saying a French word instead of a Spanish one.

 Exam tip

Remember **R**etroactive interference is when **R**ecent learning interferes with past learning.

[4 marks] | AO2 = 4

3 Simon had just returned from a motoring holiday in France, and had spent a fortnight driving on the right-hand side of the road. As he drove his car off the ferry, he saw a sign saying, 'Remember to drive on the left-hand side of the road.'

Using your knowledge of interference theory, explain why this sign might be helpful to people like Simon, who are returning to England after driving in France.

Interference theory says that we forget because _____

_____

This is especially true when _____

_____

So the reason the sign is helpful is _____

_____

4 Outline and evaluate interference theory as an explanation of forgetting.

[8 marks] | AO1 = 3 | AO3 = 5

Interference theory says we forget because _____

_____

Proactive interference is when past learning _____

_____

Retroactive interference is when recent learning _____

_____

One strength of interference theory is its application to advertising _____

_____

_____

_____

One limitation of interference theory is that some of the research it is based on is artificial.

For example _____

_____

_____

_____

Specification notes
Retrieval failure due to the absence of cues.

Year 1
Student Book
Pages 54–55

---

1 Below are four statements about retrieval failure as an explanation for forgetting. Which **one** statement is correct? Tick **one** box only.

[1 mark] AO1 = 1

A	Retrieval does not depend on a person's emotional state.	
B	Memory is more effective when there are no cues for retrieval.	
C	Retrieval failure cannot explain forgetting in the real world.	
D	The encoding specificity principle is a feature of retrieval failure.	

---

2 Outline **two** ways in which recall may be influenced by the absence of cues.

[4 marks] AO1 = 4

One way in which recall may be influenced by the absence of cues is _____

_____

For example _____

_____

Another way in which recall may be influenced by the absence of cues is _____

_____

For example _____

_____

---

3 A researcher matched ten pairs of children according to their scores on an intelligence test. The children then all listened to a brief talk about Scandinavian culture in their usual classroom. Next, one member of each matched pair remained in the classroom and answered ten questions based on the talk they had heard. The other member of each pair simultaneously answered the same questions, but in a different classroom. The average number of correct answers given by each pair is shown in the table below:

3(a) [4 marks] AO3 = 4

	Same classroom	Different classroom
Average number of correct responses given by the children	6.2	3.8

The researcher noticed that two children in the 'same classroom' condition each gave ten correct responses to the questions. All of the other children gave fewer than half this number.

(a) Explain **one** strength and **one** limitation of using a matched pairs design.

_____

_____

_____

_____

⭐ **Exam tip**

A good way of answering this question is to compare the matched pairs design with the repeated measures and independent groups designs.

(b) What is meant by the term extraneous variable?

_____

_____

_____

(c) Briefly explain how **one** extraneous variable seems to have influenced the results of this experiment.

_____

_____

_____

(d) The table indicates that more correct answers were given by the children who answered the questions in the same room as they heard the brief talk. Explain why this supports retrieval failure theory.

_____

_____

_____

(e) The researcher did not inform the participants of the purpose of the study. Explain how the researcher should have dealt with this issue.

_____

_____

_____

3(b)	[2 marks]	AO1 = 2
3(c)	[2 marks]	AO2 = 2
3(d)	[2 marks]	AO2 = 2
3(e)	[2 marks]	AO2 = 2

⭐ **Exam tip**

Remember that 'extraneous' and 'confounding' variables are not the same thing!

🐾 **Topic link**

You can find out more about dealing with ethical issues on pages 196–197 of the Year 1 Student Book.

A LEVEL ONLY

(f) The researcher believed that her questionnaire had face validity. Explain what is meant by face validity.

_____

_____

(g) The researcher wanted to see if there was a significant difference between the number of correct answers given in the two conditions. Identify an appropriate statistical test that could have been used, and give **two** reasons why the test would be appropriate.

_____

_____

_____

_____

(h) The researcher used the 5 per cent significance level. Explain why the 5 per cent significance level is normally used in psychological research.

_____

_____

3(f)	[1 mark]	AO1 = 1
3(g)	[3 marks]	AO2 = 3
3(h)	[2 marks]	AO1 = 2

4 Outline and evaluate retrieval failure due to the absence of cues as an explanation for forgetting. **[8 marks]** AO1 = 3 AO3 = 5

Retrieval failure says we forget because _____

_____

Context-dependent forgetting occurs when _____

_____

For example _____

_____

State-dependent forgetting occurs when _____

_____

For example _____

_____

_____

One strength of retrieval failure as an explanation for forgetting is its application to everyday

memory _____

_____

_____

One limitation of retrieval failure as an explanation for forgetting is that retrieval cues don't

always work _____

_____

_____

⭐ **Exam tip**

You need to make sure that each of your evaluation points links back to the question.

Specification notes
Misleading information as a factor influencing the accuracy of eyewitness testimony, including leading questions and post-event discussion.

Year 1
Student Book
Pages 56–57

[1 mark] | AO1 = 1

1 Below are four statements about the effect of misleading information on the accuracy of eyewitness testimony. Which **one** statement is correct? Tick **one** box only.

A	Post-event discussion does not influence memory.	
B	Leading questions have an effect on the accuracy of recall.	
C	Misleading information always affects the accuracy of recall.	
D	The effects of misleading information cannot be studied experimentally.	

[4 marks] | AO1 = 4

2 Outline how one research study has investigated the effects of post-event discussion on the accuracy of eyewitness testimony.

Gabbert *et al.* asked pairs of participants to watch _____

_____

Participants in one condition were asked to _____

_____

Participants in the other condition were asked to _____

_____

The researchers measured _____

_____

> ★ **Exam tip**
>
> Note the word 'how' and do not waste time writing unnecessary detail about findings and conclusions.

[4 marks] | AO2 = 4

3 A psychologist asked a group of participants questions about a film they had seen of a car being driven through the countryside. One of the questions asked how fast the car was going when it passed a 'stop' sign, even though there was no such sign in the film. A week later, the participants were asked more questions about the film, one of which was whether they had seen a 'stop' sign. Nearly a fifth of participants said that they had!

Use your knowledge of research into eyewitness testimony to explain this finding.

Research into eyewitness testimony has shown _____

_____

In this scenario, nearly a fifth of participants reported _____

_____

This can be explained by _____

_____

4 A team of psychologists was interested in the effects of misleading information on the accuracy of eyewitness testimony. Fifty university students waiting for a lecture to begin were shown a brief film of a car accident. They were then asked to complete a short questionnaire about what they had seen. Half of the participants completed questionnaires which asked if they had seen *a* broken headlight in the film. The other half completed questionnaires which asked if they had seen *the* broken headlight in the film. In fact, a broken headlight did not feature in the film. The researchers found that those asked about *the* broken headlight were more likely to have said 'yes' than those asked about *a* broken headlight.

4(a)	[1 mark]	AO1 = 1
4(b)	[3 marks]	AO3 = 3
4(c)	[1 mark]	AO2 = 1
4(d)	[2 marks]	AO3 = 2

(a) Name the experimental design used in the study described above.

_____

(b) Outline **one** limitation of this type of experimental design, and suggest **one** way in which researchers try to minimise the limitation.

_____

_____

_____

_____

(c) Name the sampling technique described in the item above.

_____

(d) Outline **one** disadvantage of the sampling technique you identified in **question (c)**.

_____

_____

_____

A LEVEL ONLY

(e) Name the level of measurement used in this study. Explain your answer.

4(e)	[2 marks]	AO2 = 2
4(f)	[1 mark]	AO2 = 1
4(g)	[1 mark]	AO2 = 1
4(h)	[2 marks]	AO1 = 2

_____

_____

(f) Name an inferential test that could have been used to analyse the data in this study.

_____

(g) The researchers found that participants were significantly more likely to incorrectly remember seeing a headlight if the word *the* was used. They used the $p<0.05$ significance level. What was the likelihood of them making a Type 1 error?

_____

(h) The findings of the study described above have been replicated by other researchers. Briefly explain **one** reason why it is important for research to be replicated.

_____

_____

⭐ **Exam tip**

A Type 1 error involves rejecting the null hypothesis when it should have been accepted. A type 2 error involves accepting the null hypothesis when it should have been rejected.

5 Discuss research into the effects of misleading information on the accuracy of eyewitness testimony.	**[12 marks]**	AO1 = 6	AO3 = 6
	[16 marks]	AO1 = 6	AO3 = 10

The suggested paragraph starters below will help form your answer:

- Loftus and Palmer asked participants to… (AO1)
- They found that… (AO1)
- Gabbert *et al* asked participants to… (AO1)
- They found that… (AO1)
- One strength of Loftus and Palmer's research comes from supporting evidence. For example Baun *et al.*… (AO3)
- One criticism of Loftus and Palmer's research is the lack of ecological validity… (AO3)
- A second criticism of Loftus and Palmer's research is the possibility of a response bias… (AO3)
- One strength of research investigating the effects of misleading information is that the findings an be applied to real life… (AO3)
- One criticism of research investigating the effects of misleading information is that witnesses differ…. (AO3)

Note: You will need some lined paper to answer this question.

 Exam tip

'Misleading information' includes leading questions and post-event discussion, so you could include either (or both).

 Topic link

Ecological validity is covered on pages 131 and 180–181 of the Year 1 Student Book.

Accuracy of eyewitness testimony: Anxiety

Specification notes
Anxiety as a factor influencing the accuracy of eyewitness testimony.

Year 1
Student Book
Pages 58–59

[1 mark] AO1 = 1

1 Below are four statements about the effect of anxiety on the accuracy of eyewitness testimony. Which **one** statement is **false**? Tick **one** box only.

A	Anxiety and the accuracy of eyewitness testimony are sometimes negatively correlated.	
B	Anxiety and the accuracy of eyewitness testimony are never correlated.	
C	Anxiety and the accuracy of eyewitness testimony are sometimes always correlated.	
D	Anxiety and the accuracy of eyewitness testimony are sometimes positively correlated.	

[4 marks] AO1 = 4

2 Describe **one** study that has investigated the effects of anxiety on the accuracy of eyewitness recall.

Johnson and Scott asked participants to _____

_____

In one condition, the participants _____

_____

In the other condition, the participants _____

_____

Johnson and Scott found _____

_____

Exam tip

For full marks, you need to explain what the researchers did and what they found.

3(a) [2 marks] AO1 = 2
3(b) [2 marks] AO3 = 2

3 Some psychologists study the effects of anxiety on eyewitness testimony in the laboratory, whereas some conduct their research in real-life settings. Instead of obtaining their own data, however, there are psychologists who use meta-analysis to study how anxiety affects eyewitness testimony.

(a) Distinguish between primary and secondary data.

_____

_____

_____

Exam tip

Think of 'primary' as 'first-hand' and 'secondary' as 'second-hand'.

(b) Outline **one** strength of laboratory experiments in psychology.

_____

_____

_____

(c) Explain how a field experiment differs from a natural experiment.

| 3(c) | [2 marks] | AO1 = 2 |
| 3(d) | [2 marks] | AO1 = 2 |

_____

_____

_____

(d) It has been claimed that field experiments have more ecological validity than laboratory experiments. Explain what is meant by the term ecological validity.

_____

_____

_____

A LEVEL ONLY

| [4 marks] | AO1 = 4 |

(e) When psychologists want to report the results of their investigations, their reports include an abstract and references. Explain the purpose of these two features of a scientific report.

_____

_____

_____

_____

---

4 Discuss research into the effects of anxiety on the accuracy of eyewitness recall.

| [12 marks] | AO1 = 6 | AO3 = 6 |
| [16 marks] | AO1 = 6 | AO3 = 10 |

The suggested paragraph starters below will help form your answer:

- Johnson and Scott asked participants to... (AO1)
- They found that... (AO1)
- Christianson and Hubinette asked participants to... (AO1)
- They found that... (AO1)
- One strength of the weapon focus effect comes from real-life studies. For example, Deffenbacher _et al._ ... (AO3)
- One criticism of the weapon focus effect is that the effect may not be caused by anxiety... (AO3)
- A second criticism of the weapon focus effect is that individual differences may play an important role in the accuracy of eyewitness testimony... (AO3)
- A third criticism of the weapon focus effect comes from an alternative theory... (AO3)
- A final criticism of the weapon focus effect comes from the results of real-life violent crimes... (AO3)

Note: You will need some lined paper to answer this question.

Exam tip

Remember to signal to the examiner when you are evaluating, by using phrases like, 'One strength of...' or 'One criticism of...'

Improving the accuracy of eyewitness testimony: The cognitive interview

Specification notes
The use of the cognitive interview in improving the accuracy of eyewitness testimony.

Year 1
Student Book
Pages 60–61

[2 marks] | AO1 = 2

1 Which **two** of the following are **not** features of the cognitive interview? Tick **two** boxes only.

A	Mental reinstatement of the original context.	
B	Recall in a different order.	
C	Collaborate with other witnesses.	
D	Recall from a changed perspective.	
E	Report only relevant information.	

🐾 Topic link

The cognitive interview is strongly linked with findings from research into retrieval failure.

[4 marks] | AO3 = 4

2 Evaluate the use of the cognitive interview.

_____

_____

_____

_____

_____

_____

⭐ Exam tip

You can choose to make one evaluative point in more detail, or two evaluation points in less detail.

[4 marks] | AO1 = 2 | AO2 = 2

3 Pete and his girlfriend were watching a reconstruction of a crime on TV. The narrator asked if anyone watching remembered a man walking a dog at the crime scene. 'Why is he asking that?' asked Pete's girlfriend, 'It's got nothing to do with the crime that was committed'.

Using your knowledge of the cognitive interview, explain to Pete's girlfriend why an apparently trivial question might be included in a reconstruction of a crime.

The cognitive interview uses the encoding specificity principle which says _____

_____

One technique the cognitive interview uses is _____

_____

So, the reason the crime reconstruction asked if anyone had seen a man walking a dog _____

_____

_____

4 Discuss the use of the cognitive interview as a way to improve the accuracy of eyewitness recall.

| [12 marks] | AO1 = 6 | AO3 = 6 |
| [16 marks] | AO1 = 6 | AO3 = 10 |

The suggested paragraph starters below will help form your answer:

- One technique that is used in the cognitive interview is... (AO1)
- The interviewer would ask the witness to... (AO1)
- Another technique that is used in the cognitive interview is... (AO1)
- The interviewer would ask the witness to... (AO1)
- The cognitive interview also uses the... technique... (AO1)
- The interviewer would ask the witness to... (AO1)
- A final technique that is used in the cognitive interview is... (AO1)
- The interviewer would ask the witness to... (AO1)
- There is research support for the effectiveness of the cognitive interview. For example, a meta-analysis....(AO3)
- One advantage of the cognitive interview is that it is particularly useful when interviewing older witnesses… (AO3)
- One problem with the cognitive interview technique concerns the information that it collects... (AO3)
- There are also problems with how the cognitive interview is used in practice. For example, Kebbell and Wagstaff... (AO3)
- A problem with evaluating the effectiveness of the cognitive interview is that, in the real world, it is a collection of related techniques, not just one 'procedure'... (AO3)

Note: You will need some lined paper to answer this question.

 Exam tip

Remember to check how many AO1 and AO3 marks are available before you start writing.

Caregiver–infant interactions

Specification notes
Caregiver–infant interactions in humans: reciprocity and interactional synchrony.

Year 1
Student Book
Pages 70–71

---

1 Which **one** of the following statements about interactional synchrony is **false**? Tick **one** box only.

[1 mark] | AO1 = 1

A	It can be seen in three-day-old infants.	
B	It is probably a learned behaviour.	
C	It is probably an innate behaviour.	
D	It isn't limited to the infant's mother.	

---

2 Explain the difference between interactional synchrony and reciprocity.

[4 marks] | AO1 = 4

SAMPLE ANSWER: *Interactional synchrony is when two people mirror what the other person is doing in their facial expressions and body movements, which includes imitating emotions. For example, if a mother smiles, and the infant smiles, too. However, reciprocity is when the mother and infant take turns to respond to each other. For example, if the mother tickles her infant, and the infant giggles in response.*

 Exam tip

Remember that when you are asked to explain a difference between two things, you need to compare them, so using words such as 'however' will help you.

---

3 Researchers conducted a controlled observational study of infant responses to adult facial expressions, such as sticking out the tongue and opening the mouth. Observers who did not know which facial expression the infant had seen watched videos of its behaviour, and recorded each time the infant stuck out its tongue and opened its mouth. After checking for inter-observer reliability, the researchers concluded that even infants as young as two weeks old imitate adult facial expressions.

3(a) | [2 marks] | AO1 = 2
3(b) | [2 marks] | AO3 = 2

(a) Explain what is meant by the term controlled observation.

_____

_____

Exam tip

You will need to say more than 'observation which is controlled' to earn marks here!

(b) Give **one** strength of using behavioural categories in observational research.

_____

_____

(c) How did the researchers attempt to control for investigator effects in the study described above?

3(c)	[2 marks]	AO2 = 2
3(d)	[2 marks]	AO1 = 2

_____

_____

(d) The researchers collected quantitative data in their study. Explain the difference between quantitative and qualitative data.

_____

_____

A LEVEL ONLY

(e) Explain what is meant by the term inter-observer reliability.

3(e)	[2 marks]	AO1 = 2
3(f)	[2 marks]	AO2 = 2
3(g)	[1 mark]	AO1 = 1

_____

_____

_____

(f) Outline **one** way in which inter-observer reliability could be assessed in the study described above.

 Exam tip

The question says 'in the study above', so don't just give a general answer about how inter-observer reliability is assessed.

_____

_____

_____

(g) Name **one** statistical test which can be used to analyse data from studies which use behavioural categories.

_____

_____

_____

---

4 Outline and evaluate research into infant–caregiver interactions.

[12 marks]	AO1 = 6	AO3 = 6
[16 marks]	AO1 = 6	AO3 = 10

The suggested paragraph starters below will help form your answer:

- Caregiver–infant interactions are characterised by… (AO1)
- The role of interactional synchrony is… (AO1)
- For example… (AO1)
- The role of reciprocity is… (AO1)
- For example… (AO1)
- Research suggests that infants' behaviour is intentional. For example… (AO3)
- Research also suggests that research into interactional synchrony can be applied to later adult relationships… (AO3)
- However, one limitation of this research in this area is that it is difficult to test infant behaviour… (AO3)
- Another limitation of research in this area is that it is hard to replicate… (AO3)
- A final limitation of research in this area is that there are individual differences… (AO3)

Note: You will need some lined paper to answer this question.

 Exam tip

If a question is worth 12 marks, you will need to make 3 evaluation points. If a question is worth 16 marks, you will need to make 4 or 5 evaluation points.

The development of attachment

Specification notes
Stages of attachment identified by Schaffer. Multiple attachments and the role of the father.

---

1 Which **one** of the following is **not** a feature of Schaffer's stages of attachment? Tick **one** box only.

[1 mark] | AO1 = 1

A	Stranger anxiety	
B	Separation anxiety	
C	Reciprocity and interactional synchrony	
D	Reunion anxiety	

---

2 Outline the role of the father in attachment.

[4 marks] | AO1 = 4

Fathers may act as primary attachment figures in that they _____

_____

Research by Heerman *et al.* found that _____

_____

Fathers may also act as secondary attachment figures in that they _____

_____

Research by Geiger *et al.* found that _____

_____

---

3 Steve is four months old. Unlike seven-month-old Anna, Steve can be comforted by anyone, and he does not seem to show any anxiety in the presence of strangers.

Identify the stage of attachment Steve is in and the stage Anna is in. Justify your choices.

[4 marks] | AO2 = 4

★ **Exam tip**

Don't forget to refer to the scenario when you justify your choice of stage for each infant.

The stage of attachment Steve is in is _____

_____

This is because he _____

_____

The stage of attachment Anna is in is _____

_____

This is because she _____

_____

4 Discuss the stages of attachment as identified by Schaffer.	**[12 marks]**	AO1 = 6	AO3 = 6
	[16 marks]	AO1 = 6	AO3 = 10

The suggested paragraph starters below will help form your answer:

- The first stage of attachment is… (AO1)
- In this stage, infants will… (AO1)
- The second stage of attachment is… (AO1)
- In this stage, infants will… (AO1)
- The third stage of attachment is… (AO1)
- In this stage, infants will… (AO1)
- The fourth stage of attachment is… (AO1)
- In this stage, infants will… (AO1)
- One limitation of this stage theory is that it suggests development is rather inflexible… (AO3)
- Another limitation of this research comes from cross-cultural studies… (AO3)
- One criticism of Schaffer's research is the importance that he places on the primary attachment figure… (AO3)
- Another criticism of Schaffer's research is that the sample he used was biased… (AO3)
- A final criticism of Schaffer's research is that his stages are based on potentially unreliable data… (AO3)

Note: You will need some lined paper to answer this question.

Animal studies of attachment

Specification notes
Animal studies of attachment: Lorenz and Harlow.

Year 1
Student Book
Pages 74–75

---

1 Which **one** of the following best describes Harlow's findings with infant rhesus monkeys? Tick **one** box only.

[1 mark] AO1 = 1

A	The infants found wire-covered surrogate mothers more comforting than cloth-covered surrogate mothers.	
B	The infants developed the strongest attachment to a surrogate mother that fed them.	
C	The infants developed the strongest attachment to a cloth-covered surrogate mother even if she was not a source of food.	
D	Motherless infants raised by a cloth-covered surrogate mother showed normal social behaviour.	

---

2 Briefly evaluate Lorenz's research into attachment.

[4 marks] AO3 = 4

One strength of Lorenz's research is _____

_____

For example, Guiton found _____

_____

However, one criticism is _____

_____

For example, Hoffman says _____

_____

Exam tip

As there are only 4 marks available, you can choose to make one evaluative point in more detail, or two evaluation points in less detail.

---

3 In Harlow's study of attachment, infant rhesus monkeys were placed in a cage in which there were two 'surrogate mothers'. One of these was made from wire and had a baby bottle attached to it. The other was made from cuddly terry cloth but did not have a baby bottle attached to it. Harlow measured how long the infants spent clinging to each surrogate mother. Shortly after Harlow's study was conducted, another researcher attempted to replicate it. Harlow had found that the infants spent longer clinging to the cloth mother. The researcher predicted that the same thing would happen in his study.

3(a)	[1 mark]	AO2 = 1
3(b)	[1 mark]	AO2 = 1

(a) Identify **one** of the independent variables in the study described above.

_____

(b) Identify the dependent variable in the study described above.

_____

Exam tip

The independent variable is directly manipulated by a research to test its effect on the dependent variable.

(c) Did the researcher who attempted to replicate Harlow's study propose a directional or non-directional hypothesis? Explain your answer.

3(c)	[3 marks]	AO2 = 3
3(d)	[4 marks]	AO3 = 4

_____

_____

_____

(d) Harlow's study was conducted in a laboratory. Explain **one** strength and **one** limitation of laboratory experiments in psychology.

 Exam tip

The question asks for a general evaluation of laboratory experiments rather than a specific evaluation of Harlow's laboratory experiments.

_____

_____

_____

_____

_____

_____

_____

A LEVEL ONLY

(e) Explain why replicability is an important feature of science.

3(e)	[2 marks]	AO1 = 2
3(f)	[1 mark]	AO2 = 1
3(g)	[2 marks]	AO1 = 2

_____

_____

(f) Name the level of measurement used in the research described above.

_____

(g) The researcher found that the monkeys spent more time on the cloth-covered surrogate mother (p<0.05). Explain what is meant by the term p<0.05.

_____

_____

_____

---

4 Discuss animal studies of attachment.

[12 marks]	AO1 = 6	AO3 = 6
[16 marks]	AO1 = 6	AO3 = 10

The suggested paragraph starters below will help form your answer:

- Lorenz investigated imprinting in goslings. He did this by… (AO1)
- Lorenz found that… (AO1)
- Harlow used rhesus monkeys to investigate whether attachment was the result of the feeding bond between mother and child… (AO1)
- He found that… (AO1)
- One strength of Lorenz's research comes from later research support. For example, Guiton found… (AO3)
- However, one criticism of Lorenz's research is his concept of imprinting… (AO3)
- One criticism of Harlow's research is the lack of control over the two 'mothers'… (AO3)
- One weakness of research with non-humans is… (AO3)
- Another weakness of research with non-humans is… (AO3)

Note: You will need some lined paper to answer this question.

 Exam tip

Your AO1 here could be limited to Harlow or Lorenz. Alternatively, you could write about the studies conducted by both of these researchers.

Specification notes
Explanations of attachment: learning theory.

Year 1
Student Book
Pages 76–77

---

① Which **one** of the following is **not** a feature of the learning theory of attachment? Tick **one** box only.

[1 mark] | AO1 = 1

A	Classical conditioning	
B	Innate predispositions	
C	Drive reduction	
D	Operant conditioning	

---

② Outline the role of learning in the development of attachment.

[4 marks] | AO1 = 4

Classical conditioning says that infants attach because they _____

_____

_____

Operant conditioning says that infants attach because they _____

_____

_____

 Exam tip

Whichever type of learning you choose to write about, remember to link your answer to the development of attachment.

---

③ A psychologist was interested in people's views about learning theory as an explanation of attachment. She wrote an article describing the theory for a local newspaper. At the end of the article, readers were asked to decide whether the theory was 'probable' or 'improbable'. Readers registered their view by ringing one of two telephone numbers. 500 people rang one of the two numbers. 21 per cent of people said the theory was 'probable' and 79 per cent said it was 'improbable'. The researcher predicted that even if people had not heard of learning theory as an explanation of attachment, they would be more likely to decide it was 'improbable' rather than 'probable'.

3(a)	[2 marks]	AO2 = 2
3(b)	[2 marks]	AO2 = 2
3(c)	[1 mark]	AO2 = 1

(a) What was the aim of the study described above?

_____

_____

_____

(b) Is the researcher's hypothesis directional or non-directional? Explain your answer.

_____

_____

_____

 Exam tip

Directional hypotheses state the direction of the predicted effect.

(c) Name the sampling technique used by the researcher.

_____

(d) Explain **one** limitation of the sampling technique you named in answer to **question (c)** above.

| 3(d) | [2 marks] | AO3 = 2 |
| 3(e) | [2 marks] | AO2 = 2 |

_____

_____

_____

(e) Explain why the data collected by the researcher is quantitative rather than qualitative.

_____

_____

_____

_____

A LEVEL ONLY

(f) Name **one** statistical test that could be used to analyse the results of this study. Give **two** reasons why this test would be appropriate.

3(f)	[3 marks]	AO2 = 3
3(g)	[2 marks]	AO2 = 2
3(h)	[2 marks]	AO1 = 2

_____

_____

_____

(g) Explain **one** way in which the validity of the researcher's study could be improved.

_____

_____

(h) Learning theory has been called a scientific theory because it is capable of being falsified. Explain what is meant by the term falsifiability in the context of science.

_____

_____

_____

	[12 marks]	AO1 = 6	AO3 = 6
4 Outline and evaluate learning theory as an explanation for attachment.			
	[16 marks]	AO1 = 6	AO3 = 10

The suggested paragraph starters below will help form your answer:

* Classical conditioning says we attach by… (AO1)
* Operant conditioning says we attach by… (AO1)
* One strength of learning theory as an explanation for attachment is that it has some explanatory power… (AO3)
* One criticism of learning theory is that a lot of the supporting research is based on non-humans… (AO3)
* A second criticism of learning theory is that it places a lot of emphasis on food… (AO3)
* A third criticism of learning theory is that drive reduction theory is outdated… (AO3)
* A final criticism of learning theory is that Bowlby's theory may provide a better explanation for attachment… (AO3)

Note: You will need some lined paper to answer this question.

Exam tip

Remember to link your explanation of learning theory to attachment.

Explanations of attachment: Bowlby's theory

Specification notes
Explanations of attachment: Bowlby's monotropic theory. The concepts of a critical period and an internal working model.

Year 1
Student Book
Pages 78–79

1 Which **one** of the following is a claim made in Bowlby's monotropic theory of attachment? Tick **one** box only.

[1 mark] AO1 = 1

A	Parents produce social releasers.	
B	There is no critical period for infants to imprint.	
C	Attachment has no survival value.	
D	Attachment in infancy acts as a template for all future relationships.	

2 Explain and briefly evaluate Bowlby's concept of a critical period.

[4 marks] AO1 = 2 AO3 = 2

A critical period is _____

_____

Bowlby thought that, in infants, this critical period _____

_____

One criticism of the idea of the critical period is _____

_____

This is a criticism because _____

_____

_____

> ⭐ **Exam tip**
>
> Remember that a critical period is a biologically determined time period during which certain characteristics can develop. If the period is 'missed', the characteristics will not develop.

3 John was reading about research into the effects of early attachment on later development. The research seemed to suggest that there was a relationship between how securely attached a child is in infancy and its emotionality in childhood and adulthood.

[4 marks] AO1 = 4

Use your knowledge of the internal working model to explain why there is a relationship between early attachment and later emotionality.

The internal working model is _____

_____

So the research John is reading about is based on _____

_____

This means that _____

_____

4 Outline and evaluate Bowlby's monotropic theory of attachment.

| [12 marks] | AO1 = 6 | AO3 = 6 |
| [16 marks] | AO1 = 6 | AO3 = 10 |

The suggested paragraph starters below will help form your answer:

- Bowlby says that we attach in order to survive. To do this, infants have an innate drive… (AO1)

- An attachment needs to form in a… (AO1)

- Social releasers… (AO1)

- Bowlby proposed that infants have one special emotional bond, which he called… (AO1)

- An internal working model is… (AO1)

- One strength of Bowlby's theory is there is research support for the idea of monotropy… (AO3)

- Another strength of Bowlby's theory is that research suggests infant attachments are adaptive. For example… (AO3)

- Further support for Bowlby's monotropic theory comes from the Minnesota parent–child study… (AO3)

- However, one criticism of Bowlby's theory is the idea of a critical period… (AO3)

- Another criticism of Bowlby's theory is that an infant's temperament may affect attachment… (AO3)

Note: You will need some lined paper to answer this question.

 Exam tip

Remember to write about Bowlby's monotropic theory, and not his theory of maternal deprivation.

Ainsworth's Strange Situation: Types of attachment

Specification notes
Ainsworth's 'Strange Situation'. Types of attachment: secure, insecure-avoidant and insecure-resistant.

Year 1
Student Book
Pages 80–81

[1 mark] AO1 = 1

1 Which **one** of the following is **not** a feature of Ainsworth's 'Strange Situation'? Tick **one** box only.

A	The infant spends time with a stranger.	
B	The stranger attempts to comfort the infant.	
C	The parent attempts to comfort the infant.	
D	The parent and stranger never interact with each other.	

[4 marks] AO1 = 4

2 Explain the difference between an insecure-avoidant and insecure-resistant attachment.

In the 'Strange Situation', when the mother leaves her child, a child who has an insecure-avoidant attachment would _____

_____

However, a child who has an insecure-resistant attachment would _____

_____

When the mother returns, the child who has an insecure-avoidant attachment would _____

_____

However, the child who has an insecure-resistant attachment would _____

_____

> ★ **Exam tip**
>
> When you are asked to explain a difference, remember to use words like 'whereas' or 'however' to make it clear you are pointing out a difference, and not just describing two things.

3(a)	[2 marks]	AO2 = 2
3(b)	[2 marks]	AO3 = 2

3 Ainsworth studied attachment types using the 'Strange Situation'. The procedure consists of eight standardised episodes, each of which lasts for three minutes. These episodes are designed to highlight behaviours such as the infant's willingness to explore and how anxious it is in the presence of a stranger. Recordings of the infant's behaviour are made by hidden observers who record what the infant is doing at 15-second intervals.

(a) Explain why research using the 'Strange Situation' is an example of controlled observation.

_____

_____

_____

(b) Give **one** limitation of controlled observation as a research method.

_____

_____

_____

> ★ **Exam tip**
>
> In controlled observation, certain variables are organised by the researcher.

(c) Distinguish between overt and covert observation.

3(c)	**[2 marks]**	AO1 = 2
3(d)	**[2 marks]**	AO2 = 2
3(e)	**[2 marks]**	AO1 = 2

_____

_____

_____

(d) Using information from the passage above, identify **two** behavioural categories used in the 'Strange Situation'.

_____

_____

_____

(e) Distinguish between event sampling and time sampling.

_____

_____

_____

A LEVEL ONLY

(f) Outline **one** way in which the reliability of the observations made in the 'Strange Situation' could be assessed.

3(f)	**[2 marks]**	AO2 = 2
3(g)	**[2 marks]**	AO1 = 2

_____

_____

(g) Ainsworth's 'Strange Situation' has been criticised for lacking ecological validity. Distinguish between ecological validity and face validity.

_____

_____

---

4 Outline and evaluate the 'Strange Situation'.

[12 marks]	AO1 = 6	AO3 = 6
[16 marks]	AO1 = 6	AO3 = 10

The suggested paragraph starters below will help form your answer:

- Ainsworth created the 'Strange Situation' to measure… (AO1)
- The procedure involves… (AO1)
- Ainsworth found that… (AO1)
- One strength of the 'Strange Situation' is that the observations were reliable… (AO3)
- Another strength of the 'Strange Situation' is that the research can be used to help improve children's lives… (AO3)
- One criticism of the 'Strange Situation' is the low level of internal validity… (AO3)
- Another criticism is that later research into attachment found… (AO3)
- A final criticism comes from research on maternal sensitivity… (AO3)

Note: You will need some lined paper to answer this question.

 Exam tip

As only 6 marks are available for AO1, it is important to keep your description of the procedure brief and to the point.

Cultural variations in attachment

Specification notes
Cultural variations in attachment, including Van IJzendoorn.

Year 1
Student Book
Pages 82–83

---

1 Which **one** of the following was found by Van IJzendoorn in his attachment research? Tick **one** box only.

[1 mark] AO1 = 1

A	Secure attachment is the norm across all cultures.	
B	Insecure-avoidant attachment is more common than insecure-resistant attachment across all cultures.	
C	Insecure-resistant attachment is more common than insecure-avoidant attachment across all cultures.	
D	The amount of secure attachment does not vary across cultures.	

---

2 Outline **one** of Van IJzendoorn's studies into cultural variations in attachment.

[4 marks] AO1 = 4

Van IJzendoorn carried out _____

_____

_____

Van IJzendoorn found _____

_____

_____

Exam tip

Although the meta-analysis of cultural variations was carried out with Kroonenberg, you can still use it to answer this question.

---

3 Sandra was watching a television documentary on how people in different cultures raise their children. Sandra noticed that Japanese children were very rarely separated from their mothers whereas German children appeared to be kept at some interpersonal distance from theirs. 'I wonder if these differences influence how securely attached these children are?', thought Sandra.

[4 marks] AO1 = 4

With reference to Van IJzendoorn's research into cross-cultural variations in attachment, outline **two** differences between German and Japanese children in terms of their attachment types.

Van IJzendoorn found that German children _____

_____

So when Sandra notices that German children _____

_____

However, Van IJzendoorn found that Japanese children _____

_____

So when Sandra notices that Japanese children _____

_____

Exam tip

When you are asked to explain a difference, remember to use words like 'whereas' or 'however' to make it clear you are pointing out a difference, and not just describing two things.

4 Discuss cultural variations in attachment.

| [12 marks] | AO1 = 6 | AO3 = 6 |
| [16 marks] | AO1 = 6 | AO3 = 10 |

The suggested paragraph starters below will help form your answer:

- Van IJzendoorn carried out… (AO1)

- Van IJzendoorn found that… (AO1)

- Grossmann and Grossmann found that… (AO1)

- Takahashi found that… (AO1)

- One strength of cross-cultural research is the development of universal principles of attachments… (AO3)

- One issue with cultural variations in attachment is that similarities may not be innately determined… (AO3)

- Another issue with cultural variations in attachments is that the findings are based on countries, not cultures… (AO3)

- A third issue with cross-cultural research is the cultural bias of attachment theory… (AO3)

- A final issue with cross-cultural research is that the research tools lack validity… (AO3)

Note: You will need some lined paper to answer this question.

 Exam tip

It is important to focus on cultural variations in attachment when answering this question, rather than simply discussing differences in other aspects of behaviour.

Bowlby's theory of maternal deprivation

Specification notes
Bowlby's theory of maternal deprivation.

Year 1
Student Book
Pages 84–85

[1 mark] AO1 = 1

1. Which **one** of the following is **not** a feature of Bowlby's theory of maternal deprivation? Tick **one** box only.

A	Maternal deprivation has long-term consequences.	
B	A good standard of physical care is the most important factor in the development of attachments.	
C	A long-term consequence of maternal deprivation is emotional maladjustment.	
D	There is a critical period in attachment formation.	

[4 marks] AO3 = 4

2. Briefly evaluate Bowlby's theory of maternal deprivation.

SAMPLE ANSWER: *One strength of Bowlby's theory of maternal deprivation is its application to childcare practices. Bowlby's work led to changes in hospitals, so now parents are allowed to stay with their children.*
However, one limitation of Bowlby's theory of maternal deprivation is that he ignores emotional separation. Just because a caregiver is physically present, doesn't mean that they are providing good emotional care, which is what his theory says children need.

Exam tip

You can write about two strengths, two limitations, or one strength and one limitation.

3(a) **[2 marks]** AO2 = 2
3(b) **[2 marks]** AO2 = 2

3. Bowlby (1944) compared 44 children who had been caught stealing (the 'thieves' group) with 44 children who were maladjusted but had not been caught stealing (the 'non-thieves' group). Most of the children and their mothers were interviewed by Bowlby, who diagnosed 14 of the 44 thieves as 'affectionless psychopaths'. Of these 14, 12 had been separated from their mothers for longer than six months. None of the 'non-thieves' group were diagnosed as 'affectionless psychopaths', and only two had experienced prolonged separation from their mothers.

(a) Calculate the percentage of 'thieves' diagnosed as 'affectionless psychopaths'. Show your calculations.

_____

_____

_____

(b) Express the number of thieves diagnosed as 'affectionless psychopaths' who had been separated from their mothers for longer than six months as a fraction of the total number of children studied by Bowlby. Show your calculations.

_____

_____

_____

Exam tip

Questions relating to mathematical skills will feature in your examination. So brush up on your percentages and fractions!

3(c)	**[2 marks]**	AO2 = 2
3(d)	**[2 marks]**	AO2 = 2
3(e)	**[2 marks]**	AO2 = 2

(c) Explain how investigator effects might have occurred in Bowlby's study.

_____

_____

_____

(d) Suggest **one** way in which investigator effects could have been avoided in Bowlby's study.

_____

_____

_____

(e) Outline **one** implication of Bowlby's research findings for the economy.

_____

_____

_____

A LEVEL ONLY

3(f)	**[4 marks]**	AO3 = 4
3(g)	**[2 marks]**	AO1 = 2
3(h)	**[2 marks]**	AO2 = 2

(f) Bowlby studied each of the children's case histories. Evaluate the use of case studies as a research method.

_____

_____

_____

_____

_____

(g) Give **one** reason why it is important for research such as Bowlby's to be replicated.

_____

_____

(h) John Bowlby's scientific report was published on pages 107–127 in volume twenty-five of the *International Journal of Psychoanalysis* in 1944. It was called 'Forty-four juvenile thieves: Their characters and home life.'

Write the full reference for this book as it should appear in the reference section of a scientific report.

_____

_____

 Exam tip

For journal articles, a suitable format is: Author's surname(s), author's initial(s), date in brackets, title of article, journal name, volume (issue number), page numbers.

4 Discuss Bowlby's theory of maternal deprivation.	**[12 marks]**	AO1 = 6	AO3 = 6
	[16 marks]	AO1 = 6	AO3 = 10

The suggested paragraph starters below will help form your answer:

- Bowlby said that prolonged separation emotional deprivation would... (AO1)
- If infants are deprived of emotional care, then they may become... (AO1)
- One strength of Bowlby's theory of maternal deprivation is... (AO3)
- Another strength of Bowlby's theory is... (AO3)
- However, one limitation of Bowlby's theory of maternal deprivation is... (AO3)
- Another limitation of Bowlby's theory is... (AO3)
- A final limitation of Bowlby's theory is... (AO3)

Note: You will need some lined paper to answer this question.

 Exam tip

Remember to write about Bowlby's maternal deprivation theory, not his monotropic theory.

Romanian orphan studies: Effects of institutionalisation

Specification notes
Romanian orphanage studies: effects of institutionalisation.

Year 1
Student Book
Pages 86–87

1 Which **one** of the following best describes the findings from studies of Romanian orphans? Tick **one** box only.

[1 mark]   AO1 = 1

A	All of the infants have recovered from institutional care.	
B	All of the infants show disinhibited attachments.	
C	There are significant social deficits in infants institutionalised beyond the age of six months.	
D	Long-term institutionalisation has little effect on either physical or social development.	

2 Outline **one** study that has investigated the effects of institutionalisation.

[4 marks]   AO1 = 4

Rutter and Sonuga-Barke examined _____

_____

_____

They found that _____

_____

_____

Exam tip

For full marks, you need to explain what the researchers did and what they found.

3 Rutter *et al.* (1998) studied 165 Romanian orphans who were adopted before the age of 43 months. The infants were 'selected at random from within bands stratified according to entry to the UK'. They were compared at 4 years and 6 years with 52 non-deprived children from the United Kingdom who had been adopted before the age of 6 months. The researchers found that were are behavioural patterns specifically associated with institutional privation.

3(a)	[2 marks]	AO1 = 2
3(b)	[2 marks]	AO3 = 2

(a) Explain what is involved in stratified sampling.

_____

_____

_____

Exam tip

In both (a) and (b) your answers do not need to be linked to Rutter et al's research.

(b) Explain **one** advantage of using a stratified sample of participants in psychological research.

_____

_____

_____

3(c) **[4 marks]**	AO3 = 4
3(d) **[2 marks]**	AO2 = 2

(c) The children underwent a standardised investigator-based interview at age 6. Explain **one** strength and **one** limitation of using interviews in psychological research.

_____

_____

_____

_____

_____

(d) The researchers defined cognitive impairment as a score of at least two standard deviations below the mean. Calculate the score that is two standard deviations below the mean when the mean is 117 and the standard deviation is 18. Show your calculations.

_____

_____

_____

A LEVEL ONLY

3(e) **[2 marks]**	AO2 = 2
3(f) **[2 marks]**	AO1 = 2
3(g) **[2 marks]**	AO1 = 2

(e) The researchers also measured autistic characteristics in the children. They used a questionnaire to do this. Outline how the researchers could assess the concurrent validity of their questionnaire.

_____

_____

(f) The researchers looked at the correlation between certain variables in their study. Name **two** statistical tests which are used to determine whether a correlation is statistically significant.

_____

_____

(g) The researchers included an abstract in the report of their investigation. Outline the purpose of the abstract in a scientific report.

_____

_____

[12 marks]	AO1 = 6	AO3 = 6
[16 marks]	AO1 = 6	AO3 = 10

4 Discuss the effects of institutionalisation.

The suggested paragraph starters below will help form your answer:

- One effect of institutionalisation is… (AO1)
- Another effect of institutionalisation is… (AO1)
- A third effect of institutionalisation is… (AO1)
- One strength of institutionalisation research is… (AO3)
- Another strength of institutionalisation research is… (AO3)
- One limitation of the Romanian orphan research is… (AO3)
- Another limitation of Romanian orphan research is… (AO3)
- A final limitation of institutionalisation research is… (AO3)

Note: You will need some lined paper to answer this question.

Exam tip

You can write about historical research studies into the effects of institutionalisation as well as contemporary research.

The influence of early attachment

Specification notes
The influence of early attachment on childhood and adult relationships, including the role of an internal working model.

Year 1
Student Book
Pages 88–89

[1 mark] AO1 = 1

1 Which **one** of the following is **not** influenced by an internal working model? Tick **one** box only.

A	Mental health	
B	Language development	
C	Romantic relationships	
D	Childhood friendships	

[4 marks] AO1 = 4

2 Explain what is meant by the term 'internal working model'.

An internal working model is _____

_____

_____

Its role is _____

_____

_____

[4 marks] AO2 = 4

3 Tim was reading a newspaper article about parents and their children. 'Blame your partner leaving you on your mum and dad!', read the headline. The article made reference to psychological research showing a correlation between attachment type in infancy and the length of a romantic relationship in adulthood. Children who were securely attached had longer-lasting romantic relationships.

Use your knowledge of research methods to explain why the author's claim that relationship breakdown in adulthood can be blamed on the type of attachment formed in infancy may be incorrect.

Correlational research is _____

_____

One limitation of correlational research is that it cannot _____

_____

However, the author claims _____

_____

This may be incorrect because _____

_____

4 Describe and evaluate the influence of early attachment on adult relationships.

| [12 marks] | AO1 = 6 | AO3 = 6 |
| [16 marks] | AO1 = 6 | AO3 = 10 |

The suggested paragraph starters below will help form your answer:

- Bowlby's theory of an internal working model says that… (AO1)
- Hazan and Shaver's 'Love Quiz' asked participants… (AO1)
- Hazan and Shaver found that… (AO1)
- One criticism of this research is… (AO3)
- Another criticism of this research is… (AO3)
- A third criticism of this research is… (AO3)
- A fourth criticism of this research is… (AO3)
- A final criticism of this research is… (AO3)

Note: You will need some lined paper to answer this question.

Definitions of abnormality

Specification notes

The statistical infrequency and deviation from social norms definitions of abnormality.

Year 1
Student Book
Pages 98–99

---

1 Which **one** of the following is a feature of the statistical infrequency definition of abnormality? Tick **one** box only.

[1 mark]   AO1 = 1

A	It takes into account how socially desirable a behaviour is.	
B	The cut-off points for identifying a behaviour as abnormal are not arbitrary.	
C	The definition is bound by culture, since a behaviour which is infrequent in one culture may be frequent in another culture.	
D	It is based on the view that statistically infrequent behaviours are always healthier than statistically frequent behaviours.	

---

2 Outline the deviation from social norms definition of abnormality.

[4 marks]   AO1 = 4

SAMPLE ANSWER: *Social norms are standards of acceptable behaviour that are set by a particular social group. Anyone who deviates from these standards is considered abnormal according to the 'deviation from social norms' definition. For example, not laughing at a funeral is an implicit social rule, so people who do laugh at funerals would be considered abnormal.*

 Exam tip

Using an example to help you explain this definition of abnormality would be a good idea.

---

3 Karim and Taliah were at a wedding. Almost everyone was dressed smartly, but one guest was wearing a t-shirt, jeans, and trainers. Karim and Taliah thought this guest was behaving abnormally, but they each had a different reason for why they thought this behaviour was abnormal.

[4 marks]   AO2 = 4

Use your knowledge of the statistical infrequency and deviation from social norms definitions to explain why Karim and Taliah thought the guest's behaviour was abnormal.

The 'statistical infrequency' definition of abnormality says that behaviour is abnormal when _____

_____

So the reason Karim and Taliah thought the guest's behaviour was abnormal is _____

_____

The 'deviation from social norms' definition of abnormality says that behaviour is abnormal when

_____

So the reason Karim and Taliah thought the guest's behaviour was abnormal is _____

_____

 Exam tip

Remember that on questions like these, it is vital that your answer is contextualised.

4 Outline and evaluate the 'statistical infrequency' definition of abnormality.

[8 marks] | AO1 = 3 | AO3 = 5

The suggested paragraph starters below will help form your answer:

- The statistical infrequency definition of abnormality says that abnormal behaviour is behaviour that… (AO1)

- For example, if someone… (AO1)

- One limitation of this definition of abnormality is that it does not take into account desirability of a statistically infrequent behaviour. For example… (AO3)

- Another limitation of the statistical infrequency definition of abnormality is that the cut-off point for where normal behaviour becomes abnormal behaviour is subjectively determined… (AO3)

Note: You will need some lined paper to answer this question.

⭐ **Exam tip**

This question requires you to show both your AO1 skills ('outline') and your AO3 skills ('evaluate').

Specification notes
The ideal mental health and failure to function adequately definitions of abnormality.

Year 1
Student Book
Pages 100–101

[1 mark]   AO1 = 1

1 Which **one** of the following is **not** an example of a criterion for 'ideal mental health'? Tick **one** box only.

A	Being able to resist stress.	
B	Behaving adaptively.	
C	Being unable to perceive reality accurately.	
D	Being independent and self-regulating.	

[4 marks]   AO3 = 4

2 Evaluate the 'failure to function adequately' definition of abnormality.

One strength of the 'failure to function adequately' definition of abnormality is that it recognises the subjective experience of the patient _____

_____

One limitation of this definition of abnormality is that some apparently dysfunctional behaviour can actually be adaptive and functional to the individual _____

_____

> ⭐ **Exam tip**
>
> As there are only 4 marks available, you can choose to make one evaluative point in more detail, or two evaluation points in less detail.

3(a)   [4 marks]   AO3 = 4

3 A researcher conducted a survey into people's beliefs about mental health. Seventy participants were given six statements, such as 'Mentally healthy people have an accurate perception of reality' and 'Mentally healthy people can deal with stress'. Participants were asked to indicate whether they thought each statement was true or false. The table below shows the results for the statement about dealing with stress:

	Number saying 'true'	Number saying 'false'
'Mentally healthy people can deal with stress'	42	28

(a) The participants could only answer 'true' or 'false' to each statement. Explain **one** strength and **one** limitation of this approach to conducting a survey.

_____

_____

_____

_____

_____

> ⭐ **Exam tip**
>
> You will receive one mark for a basic explanation of a strength/limitation, and a further mark if you elaborate the explanation perhaps by using an example.

(b) Write **one** other statement that could have been used in the survey. Explain why this would be a suitable statement.

_____

_____

_____

(c) What percentage of the participants believed the statement about stress was true? Show your calculations.

_____

_____

(d) Express the number of participants saying 'false' as a fraction of the total number of participants. Show your calculations.

_____

_____

(e) In a follow-up study, the researcher used an unstructured interview to ask participants about the responses they had given to the statements. Explain **one** limitation of using unstructured interviews in psychological research.

_____

_____

_____

_____

3(b)	[2 marks]	AO2 = 2
3(c)	[2 marks]	AO2 = 2
3(d)	[2 marks]	AO2 = 2
3(e)	[2 marks]	AO3 = 2

A LEVEL ONLY

(f) Identify the level of measurement used in this study. Explain your answer.

_____

(g) Name an appropriate statistical test that could be used to analyse the data in the table above. Apart from reference to the level of measurement, give **two** reasons why this test would be appropriate.

_____

_____

_____

_____

3(f)	[2 marks]	AO2 = 2
3(g)	[3 marks]	AO2 = 3

⭐ **Exam tip**

'Apart from' means that you have to give other reasons why a particular statistical test would be appropriate.

4 Discuss **two** definitions of abnormality.

| [12 marks] | AO1 = 6 | AO3 = 6 |
| [16 marks] | AO1 = 6 | AO3 = 10 |

The suggested paragraph starters below will help form your answer:

- The 'deviation from ideal mental health' definition of abnormality explains abnormality as ... (AO1)

- An example of a behaviour that would be considered abnormal under this definition would be ... (AO1)

- One strength of the 'deviation from ideal mental health' definition of abnormality is ... (AO3)

- One limitation of the 'deviation from ideal mental health' definition of abnormality is ...(AO3)

- The 'failure to function adequately' definition of abnormality explains abnormality as ...(AO1)

- An example of a behaviour that would be considered abnormal under this definition would be ... (AO1)

- One strength of the 'failure to function adequately' definition of abnormality is ...(AO3)

- One problem with this definition of abnormality is that some apparently dysfunctional behaviour can actually be functional for the individual ... (AO3)

Note: You will need some lined paper to answer this question.

 Exam tip

If a question is worth 12 marks, you will need to make at least 3 evaluation points. If a question is worth 16 marks, you will need to make 4 or 5 evaluation points.

Mental disorders

Year 1
Student Book
Pages 102–103

Specification notes

The behavioural, emotional, and cognitive characteristics of phobias, depression, and obsessive-compulsive disorder (OCD).

---

1 Which **two** of the following are characteristics of depression? Tick **two** boxes only.

[2 marks] | AO1 = 2

A	A feeling of control over the environment.	
B	Reduced or increased activity levels.	
C	Increased self-esteem.	
D	Negative self-concept.	
E	Increased pleasure in social activities.	

---

2 Explain the difference between obsessions and compulsions.

[4 marks] | AO1 = 4

An obsession is _____

_____

For example, someone with OCD might have an obsession with _____

_____

However, a compulsion is _____

_____

For example, someone with OCD might _____

_____

> **Exam tip**
>
> Remember that when you are asked to explain a difference, you need to compare the two, so using words such as 'however' will help you.

---

3 Brian finds it difficult to fly on aeroplanes. He can't remember any of the safety instructions given before the flight because he says his 'mind is elsewhere'. When the engines roar, Brian panics. All he wants to do is get off the plane as quickly as possible.

[6 marks] | AO2 = 6

Identify the behavioural, cognitive, and emotional characteristics of phobias as shown by Brian in this description.

One behavioural characteristic of phobias is _____

_____

For example, Brian _____

_____

One cognitive characteristic of phobias is _____

_____

For example, Brian _____

_____

One emotional characteristic of phobias is _____

_____

For example, Brian _____

_____

> **Exam tip**
>
> This question is about 'Brian', so you must use the information in the item when you answer this question.

The behavioural approach to explaining phobias

Specification notes
The two-process model, including classical and operant conditioning.

Year 1
Student Book
Pages 104–105

1 Which **one** of the following is **not** a feature of the behavioural approach to explaining phobias? Tick **one** box only.

[1 mark] AO1 = 1

A	The claim that phobias can be acquired through classical conditioning.	
B	The claim that generalisation of a conditioned response rarely occurs with phobias.	
C	The claim that negative reinforcement can explain the maintenance of phobias.	
D	The claim that phobias can be acquired through modelling the behaviour of others.	

Topic link

The behavioural approach is also included in the Approaches topic on pages 126–127 of the Year 1 Student Book.

2 Outline **one** limitation of the behavioural approach to explaining phobias.

[3 marks] AO3 = 4

One limitation of the behavioural approach to explaining phobias is _____

_____

For example, DiNardo *et al.* found _____

_____

The diathesis-stress model says that we inherit _____

_____

This suggests that _____

_____

Exam tip

One way to develop each of your evaluation points is to use the **PEEL** (**P**oint, **E**vidence, **E**xplain, **L**ink) approach.

3 When Sally was five, she had her first filling at the dentist. The dentist's drill hit a nerve and was very painful. Ever since then, Sally has been afraid of going to the dentist. When Sally has a dental appointment, she cannot go through the surgery door. She tells her friends that walking away gives her an amazing sense of relief.

[6 marks] AO2 = 6

Use the two-process model to explain what could have caused Sally's phobia and why she continues to avoid going to the dentist.

Classical conditioning occurred here, as the unconditioned stimulus was the nerve being hit,

leading to _____

_____

A visit to the dentist becomes _____

_____

Operant conditioning says that we learn by _____

_____

Every time Sally walks away from the dentist's door, she feels _____

_____

This would maintain Sally's phobia because _____

_____

Exam tip

The two-process model includes both classical conditioning and operant conditioning, so remember to include both in your answer.

4 Discuss the behavioural approach to explaining phobias.

| [12 marks] | AO1 = 6 | AO3 = 6 |
| [16 marks] | AO1 = 6 | AO3 = 10 |

The suggested paragraph starters below will help form your answer:

- The behavioural approach says that we acquire phobias through classical conditioning... (AO1)

- This says that unconditioned stimulus (e.g. a loud noise) leads to an unconditioned response of fear. If a neutral stimulus (e.g. a rat) is paired with... (AO1)

- The behavioural approach says that our phobia is maintained due to operant conditioning... (AO1)

- If a behaviour is negatively reinforced then it is more likely to be repeated. So if someone avoids the phobic stimulus, this reduces fear... (AO1)

- One strength of the behavioural approach is that some people can recall a specific event that led to their phobia developing. For example, Sue *et al.* found... (AO3)

- One limitation of the behavioural approach is that it cannot explain the development of all phobias... (AO3)

- Another limitation of this approach is that a phobia doesn't always develop after a traumatic incident... (AO3)

- A final limitation of the behavioural approach is that it ignores the cognitive aspects of the phobia's development... (AO3)

- A better explanation for the development of phobias may be biological preparedness... (AO3)

Note: You will need some lined paper to answer this question.

Exam tip

If you do not link your explanation of the behavioural approach to phobias, you won't gain many AO1 marks.

The behavioural approach to treating phobias

Specification notes
Systematic desensitisation, including relaxation and use of hierarchy; flooding.

Year 1
Student Book
Pages 106–107

[1 mark] AO1 = 1

1 Which **one** of the following is a feature of systematic desensitisation? Tick **one** box only.

A	Disputing irrational beliefs about a phobic stimulus.	
B	A single session of experiencing the phobic stimulus at its worst.	
C	Reducing anxiety by the gradual introduction of psychotherapeutic drugs.	
D	Using relaxation techniques as part of the therapeutic process.	

[4 marks] AO1 = 4

2 Explain how systematic desensitisation differs from flooding.

Systematic desensitisation is _____

_____

However, in flooding _____

_____

⭐ **Exam tip**

Remember that when you are asked to explain a difference between two things, you need to compare them, so using words such as 'however' will help you.

[4 marks] AO1 = 4

3 Gordon is afraid of snow. Gordon's children are excited about going on a skiing holiday with their father. Gordon doesn't want to let his children down, so he asks a friend, who is a clinical psychologist, for some advice. His friend recommends that Gordon uses flooding to overcome his fears.

Explain how flooding could be used to treat Gordon's fear of snow.

Flooding involves a single exposure to the most feared situation. First, Gordon would learn _____

_____

_____

Then he would be put in the most feared situation. For example _____

_____

_____

As adrenaline levels naturally decrease, Gordon will _____

_____

⭐ **Exam tip**

Remember that the person put in their most feared situation cannot avoid confronting the phobic stimulus.

4 Discuss the behavioural approach to treating phobias.

| [12 marks] | AO1 = 6 | AO3 = 6 |
| [16 marks] | AO1 = 6 | AO3 = 10 |

The suggested paragraph starters below will help form your answer:

- Systematic desensitisation treats phobias by... (AO1)

- Flooding treats phobias by... (AO1)

- One advantage of using systematic desensitisation to treat phobias is that it has been found to be successful... (AO3)

- One problem with systematic desensitisation is that it is not appropriate for all phobias... (AO3)

- One strength of flooding as a way to treat phobias is that it is effective as long as the patient sticks to it... (AO3)

- One problem with flooding is that it can be an unethical way to treat someone with a phobia... (AO3)

- A final problem with both of these therapies is that they only remove the symptoms of a phobia, not the causes of it... (AO3)

Note: You will need some lined paper to answer this question.

Exam tip

You would need approximately 180 words for your AO1, and 180 words for AO3 (if it's worth 12 marks), or 300 words (if it's worth 16 marks).

The cognitive approach to explaining depression

Specification notes
Beck's negative triad and Ellis' ABC model.

[1 mark] | AO1 = 1

1 Which **one** of the following is **not** a feature of Beck's negative triad or Ellis' ABC model cognitive approaches to explaining depression? Tick **one** box only.

A	Mustabatory thinking	
B	Positive schemas	
C	The negative triad	
D	Diathesis–stress	

 Topic link

The cognitive approach is also included in the Approaches topic on pages 130–131 of the Year 1 Student Book.

[4 marks] | AO1 = 4

2 Outline **either** Beck's negative triad **or** Ellis' ABC model explanation for depression.

Beck says depression occurs because _____

_____

He talks about a negative triad, which is _____

_____

_____

OR

Ellis says depression occurs because _____

_____

His ABC model says _____

_____

_____

 Exam tip

If you write about both Beck's *and* Ellis' explanations, then you will only receive credit for one.

3(a) | **[2 marks]** | AO2 = 2
3(b) | **[2 marks]** | AO2 = 2

3 A psychologist devised a questionnaire to assess people's interpretations of events described in brief stories. She hypothesised that there would be a positive correlation between scores on Beck's Depression Inventory and the tendency to select to the most negative interpretation of the events depicted in the stories. A statistical test indicated that there was a significant correlation, and the researcher concluded that her study supported the view that there are cognitive biases in depression.

(a) The questionnaire used open questions. Explain **one** strength of using open questions on this questionnaire.

_____

_____

_____

(b) Was the psychologist's hypothesis directional or non-directional? Explain your answer.

_____

_____

_____

Exam tip

A non-directional hypothesis predicts that there is no difference or correlation without stating the direction of the difference or correlation.

3(c)	[2 marks]	AO3 = 2
3(d)	[2 marks]	AO2 = 2
3(e)	[2 marks]	AO2 = 2

(c) The psychologist used volunteers for this study. Outline **one** disadvantage of using volunteers as participants in psychological research.

_____

_____

_____

(d) The participants' responses were analysed by the psychologist herself. Briefly explain how this could have led to investigator effects occurring in this study.

_____

_____

_____

(e) Outline **one** way in which the psychologist could have avoided the possibility of investigator effects in her study.

_____

_____

_____

A LEVEL ONLY

3(f)	[1 marks]	AO2 = 1
3(g)	[4 marks]	AO1 = 4

(f) Name **one** statistical test that could have been used to determine whether or not the correlation was significant.

_____

(g) The psychologist believed that her questionnaire had face validity. Identify and outline **two** other types of validity in psychological research.

_____

_____

_____

_____

⭐ Exam tip

The specification identifies concurrent, ecological, and temporal as other types of validity you could be asked about.

	[12 marks]	AO1 = 6	AO3 = 6
4 Outline and evaluate the cognitive approach to explaining depression.	[16 marks]	AO1 = 6	AO3 = 10

The suggested paragraph starters below will help form your answer:

*   The cognitive approach explains depression as being a result of... (AO1)
*   Ellis says that... (AO1)
*   Beck says that... (AO1)
*   One strength of the cognitive approach to explaining depression is that it is supported by research... (AO3)
*   Another strength of this approach is that it focuses on the person, giving them responsibility for their disorder... (AO3)
*   A third strength of the cognitive approach to explaining depression is that it has useful real-life applications. For example... (AO3)
*   One limitation of the cognitive explanations of depression is that not all irrational beliefs are in fact irrational, but may only seem that way... (AO3)
*   A second limitation of the cognitive explanations of depression is that it is very likely that genetic factors and neurotransmitters are involved in depression... (AO3)

Note: You will need some lined paper to answer this question.

The cognitive approach to treating depression

Specification notes
Cognitive behaviour therapy (CBT), including challenging irrational thoughts.

Year 1
Student Book
Pages 110–111

1 Which **one** of the following best describes the aims of cognitive behaviour therapy? Tick **one** box only.

[1 mark] AO1 = 1

A	To return neurotransmitter levels to normal.	
B	To identify the brain structures involved in depression.	
C	To challenge irrational beliefs and replace them with more rational beliefs.	
D	To develop new ways of increasing anxiety.	

2 Describe how challenging irrational thoughts can be used as a treatment for depression.

[4 marks] AO1 = 4

SAMPLE ANSWER: *Ellis' rational emotive behaviour therapy focuses on challenging irrational thoughts and replacing them with effective rational beliefs which produce new feelings. It does this by using things like empirical disputing, which asks for proof that someone's belief is accurate. It also uses pragmatic disputing which emphasises the uselessness of self-defeating, by asking how the belief is likely to be helpful to the person. Clients may be asked to complete assignments between sessions, which helps them to test their irrational beliefs against reality, and putting new rational beliefs into practice.*

 Exam tip

Notice the word 'how' and do not waste time writing unnecessary detail about why the therapy might be effective.

3 A researcher was interested in the effects of cognitive therapy for depression. She randomly allocated participants to either a treatment condition or a control condition. At the end of the trial, changes in the participants' self-rated depression scores were compared.

3(a)	[2 marks]	AO2 = 2
3(b)	[1 mark]	AO2 = 1
3(c)	[2 marks]	AO1 = 2

(a) Identify the dependent variable in this study.

_____

_____

_____

(b) Name the experimental design used in this study.

_____

(c) Describe **one other** experimental design that researchers use in psychology.

_____

_____

_____

Exam tip

When you see Experimental Design, remember 'Really Interesting Method' (Repeated, Independent, and Matched Pairs).

(d) Outline **one** way in which participants could have been randomly allocated to the treatment and control conditions.

| 3(d) | [3 marks] | AO2 = 3 |
| 3(e) | [2 marks] | AO1 = 2 |

_____

_____

_____

_____

★ **Exam tip**

Be detailed in your outline here. 'Tossing a coin' isn't an 'outline'!

(e) Explain why it is important to randomly allocate participants to conditions in a psychological study.

_____

_____

_____

_____

A LEVEL ONLY

| 3(f) | [2 marks] | AO1 = 2 |
| 3(g) | [3 marks] | AO1 = 3 |

(f) The researcher found a significant difference between the treatment and control conditions. The difference was significant at p<0.01. What is meant by 'the difference was significant at p<0.01'?

_____

_____

(g) What is meant by a Type 1 error? Explain why psychologists normally use the 0.05 level of significance in their research.

_____

_____

_____

_____

---

4 Discuss the cognitive approach to treating depression.

| [12 marks] | AO1 = 6 | AO3 = 6 |
| [16 marks] | AO1 = 6 | AO3 = 10 |

The suggested paragraph starters below will help form your answer:

- Ellis' rational emotive behaviour therapy focuses on... (AO1)
- It does this by disputing irrational thoughts and beliefs. For example... (AO1)
- Clients might be asked to... (AO1)
- One strength is that research shows Ellis' rational emotive behaviour therapy is effective... (AO3)
- The cognitive approach's claim that changing people's behaviour can go some way to treating their depression is also supported by research into the beneficial effects of exercise... (AO3)
- One weakness of cognitive behavioural therapy is that it may not be suitable for some people... (AO3)
- Another weakness of cognitive approaches to therapy is that research suggests there isn't much evidence between different psychotherapies' effectiveness... (AO3)
- A final weakness of cognitive behavioural therapy is that drug therapies may be a more appropriate therapy for some people... (AO3)

Note: You will need some lined paper to answer this question.

The biological approach to explaining OCD

Specification notes

Genetic and neural explanations.

[1 mark] | AO1 = 1

1 Below are four statements about the biological approach to explaining OCD. Which **one** statement is correct? Tick **one** box only.

A	Genetic factors do not play a role in OCD.	
B	Serotonin levels are abnormally high in OCD.	
C	Serotonin and dopamine levels are abnormally low in OCD.	
D	An abnormality in certain brain structures is linked to OCD.	

 Topic link

The biological approach is also included in the Approaches topic on pages 132–133 of the Year 1 Student Book.

[4 marks] | AO1 = 4

2 Outline the biological approach to explaining OCD.

The genetic approach to explaining OCD says that _____

_____

The COMT gene regulates _____

_____

The SERT gene regulates _____

_____

In patients with OCD, serotonin levels are _____

_____

In patients with OCD, dopamine is thought to be _____

_____

 Exam tip

You can choose to write about one biological explanation in more detail, or two explanations in less detail.

[4 marks] | AO1 = 2 | AO2 = 2

3 A psychologist conducted a study using identical twins. She found that if one member of a twin pair had been diagnosed with OCD, there was a 65 per cent chance that the other twin had received the same diagnosis.

Using the data in the item above, explain why some psychologists would argue that the biological approach is a useful way of explaining the causes of OCD.

A concordance rate is _____

_____

Here, the concordance rate is 65 per cent so it suggests that _____

_____

_____

_____

This means that _____

_____

	[12 marks]	AO1 = 6	AO3 = 6
	[16 marks]	AO1 = 6	AO3 = 10

4 Outline and evaluate the biological approach to explaining OCD.

The suggested paragraph starters below will help form your answer:

- The biological approach to explaining OCD says that... (AO1)
- The COMT gene regulates... (AO1)
- The SERT gene regulates... (AO1)
- OCD may be the result of biochemical abnormalities in the brain. For example... (AO1)
- OCD may also be the result of brain damage. For example... (AO1)
- One strength of the biological approach to explaining OCD is that there is support from family studies for the idea that genes play a role in OCD... (AO3)
- Another strength of the biological approach is that brain scans indicate patients with OCD show heightened activity in their orbitofrontal cortex... (AO3)
- A third strength of the biological approach to explaining OCD is that twin studies also support the idea that genes play a role in OCD... (AO3)
- A final strength of the biological approach is that research shows that there is a genetic link to abnormal neurotransmitter levels... (AO3)
- However, one limitation of the biological approach is that psychological explanations might be better... (AO3)

Note: You will need some lined paper to answer this question.

The biological approach to treating OCD

Specification notes
Drug therapy.

[1 mark] | AO1 = 1

1 Which **one** of the following statements about drug therapy is **false**? Tick **one** box only.

A	Drugs used to treat OCD have side effects.	
B	Drugs used to treat OCD are not a lasting cure.	
C	Drugs used to treat OCD reduce anxiety by decreasing serotonin levels.	
D	Drugs used to treat OCD are also used to treat other disorders.	

[4 marks] | AO3 = 4

2 Explain **one** strength of the biological approach to treating OCD.

SAMPLE ANSWER: *One strength of the biological approach to treating OCD is that drugs require little input or effort from the user. Psychological therapies are time consuming, and require the person to attend meetings and think about tackling their problems. Drug therapies don't do this, and so they are more economical to the health service.*

3(a)	[2 marks]	AO1 = 2
3(b)	[2 marks]	AO1 = 2
3(c)	[4 marks]	AO2 = 4

3 A research team conducted a meta-analysis of studies looking at the effectiveness of antidepressants in treating OCD. They included only studies in which participants had been randomly assigned to conditions, and in which an attempt had been made to minimise demand characteristics and investigator effects. They also only analysed studies which had been published in peer-reviewed journals.

(a) The investigation above is based on secondary data. Explain what is meant by 'secondary data'.

_____

_____

(b) The research team included only studies in which there had been an attempt to minimise demand characteristics. Explain what is meant by the term demand characteristics.

_____

_____

_____

(c) Briefly explain how investigator effects might occur in studies such as the one described above, and outline how they could be avoided in these studies.

_____

_____

_____

_____

(d) The research team analysed only studies which had been published in peer-reviewed journals. Explain **one** reason why it is important for research to undergo a peer-review process.

3(d)	[2 marks]	AO1 = 2

_____

_____

_____

A LEVEL ONLY

(e) Some of the studies included in the research team's meta-analysis were replications of other research. Outline **one** reason why it is important for research to be replicated.

3(e)	[2 marks]	AO1 = 2
3(f)	[2 marks]	AO1 = 2
3(g)	[2 marks]	AO2 = 2

_____

_____

(f) In the report of their investigation, the researchers included an abstract. Explain the purpose of an abstract in the report of a psychological investigation.

_____

_____

(g) Pete Smith and Margaret Brown published a book based on their meta-analysis. It was called *Are Drugs Effective in Treating OCD?*, and was published in Oxford in 2017 by Oxford University Press. Another psychologist wants to include a reference to Smith and Brown's book in her own scientific report.

Write the full reference for Smith and Brown's book as it should appear in the reference section of the psychologist's own report.

_____

_____

 Exam tip

For books, a suitable format is: Author's surname(s), author's initial(s), date in brackets, title of book, place of publication, publisher.

---

4 Outline and evaluate the biological approach to treating OCD.

[12 marks]	AO1 = 6	AO3 = 6
[16 marks]	AO1 = 6	AO3 = 10

The suggested paragraph starters below will help form your answer:

- One type of drug that can be used to treat OCD is an SSRI. These work by... (AO1)
- Tricyclics are another type of drug that can be used to treat OCD. These work by... (AO1)
- One strength of drug therapy is that there is research evidence that it is effective in treating OCD... (AO3)
- Another strength of drug therapy is that it requires little input or effort from the user... (AO3)
- One limitation of drug therapy as a treatment for OCD is that drugs have unpleasant side effects... (AO3)
- A second limitation with drug therapy is that drugs are not a lasting cure for people with OCD... (AO3)
- A final limitation of drug therapy is that there is a publication bias in research... (AO3)

Note: You will need some lined paper to answer this question.

 Exam tip

One way to develop your evaluation points is to use the **PEEL** (**P**oint, **E**vidence, **E**xplain, **L**ink) approach.

Notes

The Complete Companions

Psychology A Level and AS Paper 1

Authors
Clare Compton, Rob McIlveen

Series Editor
Mike Cardwell

From the team that brought you the best-selling and trusted **The Complete Companions,** **The Complete Companions Exam Workbooks** provide students with skills-building activities and step-by-step exam-style practice questions to ensure they approach their exams confident of success. They are completely matched to AQA's AS and A Level examination requirements and ideal for use in class or for homework and revision.

This **A Level and AS Paper 1 Exam Workbook** covers the four compulsory topics examined by A Level Paper 1: **Social influence**, **Memory**, **Attachment** and **Psychopathology**. It also covers the three compulsory topics examined by AS Level Paper 1: **Social influence**, **Memory** and **Attachment**, and one of the three compulsory topics examined by AS Level Paper 2: **Psychopathology**.

- Complete match to both the popular **The Complete Companions** series and the specification, so you can trust that you've covered everything you need to practise.

- Draws on **key issues from examiner reports**, so you can be confident that it reflects exactly what is required for success at both AS and A Level.

- Focussed **exam advice and tips** throughout, with suggested **AO1/AO2/AO3 mark allocations** to help structure answers.

Also available:

Paper 2 Exam
Workbook for AQA
978-019-842891-6

Paper 3 Exam
Workbook for
AQA: Relationships
including Issues and
debates
978-019-842895-4

Paper 3 Exam
Workbook for AQA:
Gender including
Issues and debates
978-019-842894-7

Paper 3 Exam
Workbook for AQA:
Schizophrenia
978-019-842896-1

Paper 3 Exam
Workbook for AQA:
Aggression
978-019-842892-3

Paper 3 Exam
Workbook for AQA:
Forensic psychology
978-019-842893-0

Exam-style practice questions for each topic, ramped from lower tariff to essay style

Marks clearly presented with suggested breakdown of Assessment Objectives

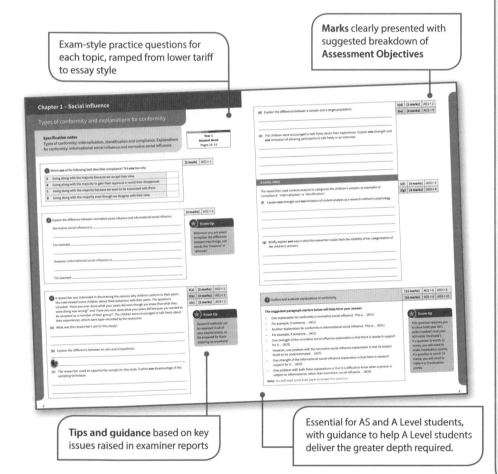

Tips and guidance based on key issues raised in examiner reports

Essential for AS and A Level students, with guidance to help A Level students deliver the greater depth required.

Answers can be found at **www.oxfordsecondary.co.uk/completecompanionsanswers**

OXFORD
UNIVERSITY PRESS

How to get in touch:
web   www.oxfordsecondary.co.uk
email   schools.enquiries.uk@oup.com
tel   01536 452620
fax   01865 313472

ISBN 978-0-19-842890-9

9 780198 428909